COOKING WITH
Bon Appétit

COOKING WITH
Bon Appétit

Breakfasts and Brunches

THE KNAPP PRESS
Publishers
Los Angeles

Copyright © 1983 by Knapp Communications Corporation

Published by The Knapp Press
5455 Wilshire Boulevard, Los Angeles, California 90036

Library of Congress Cataloging in Publication Data

Main entry under title:

Cooking with Bon appétit.

    Includes index.
     1. Breakfasts   2. Brunches.   I. Bon appétit.
II. Title: Breakfasts and brunches.
TX733.C684   1983   641.5'2   82-23308
ISBN 0-89535-115-3

On the cover: *Oranges Orientale, Baked Egg Custard with Onion and Bacon, Seared Chicken Livers with Chives, Basic Croissants*

Printed and bound in the United States of America

10 9 8 7 6 5 4 3 2

🍂 Contents

Foreword . . . . *vii*

1 Eggs, Soufflés and Quiches 1
Whole Eggs   2
Scrambled Eggs and Omelets   6
Soufflés and Mousselines   14
Quiches and Tarts   19

2 Seafood, Poultry and Meat Entrées 35
Seafood   36
Poultry   38
Meats   40

3 Pancakes, Breads and Pastries 49
Sweet Pancakes, Waffles and Toasts   50
Savory Pancakes and Crepes   56
Quick Breads and Muffins   62
Yeast Breads and Cakes   67
Pastries   76

4 Vegetable Side Dishes 85
Casseroles and Sautés   86
Salads, Sorbets and Spreads   89

5 Sweet Side Dishes 93
Fruits   94
Sorbets   98
Spreads and Sauces   102

6 Beverages 105
Juices and Dairy Drinks   106
Cold Punches and Cocktails   107
Hot Drinks   109

Index 115

❦ Foreword

No meal offers more opportunity for surprise and delight than breakfast. And on weekends and holidays, the purely American invention of the late morning meal known as brunch presents a joyously relaxed occasion for entertaining. Inspired by these two meals, we've gathered together over 200 of our favorite breakfast and brunch recipes from the pages of *Bon Appétit*. All have been tested in our kitchens; all are so tempting that cold cereal and milk may vanish from your table for years.

To make menu planning easier for either breakfasts or brunches, the six chapters here are organized by main ingredient. As eggs are a featured ingredient in many morning meals, the volume begins with a delightful variety of egg-based dishes—from The Perfect Eggs Benedict (page 2) to a Fantasy Quiche rich with cream cheese and fresh mushrooms (page 20). It then continues with chapters on hearty main courses such as Seafood Strudel (page 36); pancakes and breads such as Herb Crepes Bernoise (page 59) and Petits Pains au Chocolat (page 71); and side dishes, both savory vegetable—Poached Leeks in Sauce Verte (page 89), perhaps—and sweet, such as a spicy Winter Compote (page 98). The book concludes with a section on appropriate morning beverages, either as cold and bracing as a Clam Bloody Mary (page 107) or as hot and cheering as The Bishop (page 111), a mulled wine perfect for winter brunches. And throughout, you will find the tips that lead to perfection—from making your own sourdough starter (pages 52–53) to how best to poach or boil an egg (pages 4–5) or brew memorable pots of coffee or tea (pages 110–113).

Throughout the book, you will find recipes for all kinds of breakfasts or brunches, from quick meals before work to leisurely weekend feasts. On busy mornings you might choose Kentucky Scrambled Eggs (page 6) or Sprout Peanut Omelet (page 9), served, perhaps, with Homemade Sausage Patties (page 41) and Pumpkin Apple Bundt Bread (page 62). Better suited to a slower-paced weekend morning is a special recipe such as Deep Dish Chili Cheese Pie (page 25) served with Champagne Sausage (page 43). An impeccable brunch menu can be as simple as the Classic Omelet (page 7), for example, followed by Almond Combs (page 77) and coffee. For a sophisticated brunch as elegant and enticing as a festive luncheon, Cold Samon with Avocado Cream (page 36) is an irresistible main course; Cheese Croissants (page 72) and a refreshing Cucumber Sorbet (page 90) make appropriately elegant accompaniments. A Russian Grandma's Cheese Blintzes (page 53), served with Strawberry-Filled Cantaloupe (page 95) make a homey and heartening start to the day.

Taking the day's first meal out of the doldrums brings many benefits. Heavenly aromas from the kitchen work miracles on sleepy heads; the spare few minutes spent cooking instead of cajoling are doubly profitable. Good beginnings promise better performances throughout the day for everyone. And sharing the bounty with friends at weekends is a loving gesture that brings its own rewards. Bon appétit.

1 ❦ Eggs, Soufflés and Quiches

While evolutionary historians may still be debating whether the egg preceded the chicken or followed it, there is absolutely no question which comes first at the breakfast and brunch table. Eggs are supreme on almost every morning menu, and with very good reason: They lend themselves to a staggering variety of dishes, virtually all of which are easy to prepare.

In this chapter we have put all different kinds of egg recipes in one basket, so to speak. First are dishes using whole eggs—poached, baked, boiled and broiled. Poached eggs star in The Perfect Eggs Benedict (page 2) and in several variations on that classic. Hard-boiled eggs take on an Italian flavor in Trattoria Eggs (see page 6); and from Mexico there are Huevos en Cazuela (page 3), in which the eggs are broiled with cheese and two kinds of chilies.

As varied as whole-egg dishes may be, an entirely new realm of possibilities opens up with scrambled eggs and omelets. There are classic plain omelets, puffy omelets and omelets with many kinds of fillings—from onions to shrimp and mushrooms to sprouts and peanuts. Then there are the variations on the theme: omelet pancakes, an omelet loaf that combines eggs and sourdough bread, and the slow-cooked Italian frittata. A bit fancier is the Spinach Turban (page 12), a phyllo-layered centerpiece that can be made a day ahead.

The elegant soufflé was once considered a tricky dish, but modern kitchen equipment and temperature controls have rendered it almost foolproof. Rich and delightfully puffy, soufflés can be flavored in myriad ways; here you'll find recipes for soufflés enhanced with beer and cheese, with asparagus and yogurt, cauliflower and watercress, oysters and spinach, sweet potato, and more.

An international collection of quiches, tarts and tourtes rounds out our egg recipes, and by whatever name you call them, these savory egg-based pies have become a brunch and breakfast standby. They are as variable as the soufflé and extremely easy to prepare. Most can be a meal in themselves and—a bonus for the busy cook—they can be made ahead and served cold or at room temperature.

The standard question is, "How would you like your eggs?" Here is a basketful of answers.

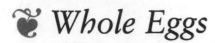 Whole Eggs

The Perfect Eggs Benedict

French egg poachers made of tin, with an egg-shaped, slotted receptacle for the egg and four little legs to stand in the simmering water, are fun to use and shape the eggs nicely. Be sure to butter the receptacle lightly before breaking your egg into it.

American egg poachers—those round, tin mini-double-boiler affairs with covers—are not desirable because they steam the eggs instead of poaching.

4 servings

8 **fresh large eggs**
4 **English muffins, split**
8 **slices Virginia ham, cut into rounds to fit neatly over muffins**
1 **cup Hollandaise Sauce, or to taste (see following recipe)**

8 **thin slices black truffle (optional garnish)**
Watercress or parsley (garnish)

Here are the five steps to making The Perfect Eggs Benedict:

1.   Poach the eggs and place in a warm-water bath.
2.   Grill the ham slices, drain, and keep warm in an oven with the heat turned to very low, or in a toaster-oven on low.
3.   Prepare the hollandaise sauce and keep it warm.
4.   Toast split English muffins, lay a slice of ham on each half, lift the poached eggs out of the warm water, drain them on a napkin or towel and place atop the warm ham.
5.   Spoon the hollandaise sauce to cover each of the eggs, garnish with a slice of black truffle and with either a sprig of watercress or parsley.

Poaching the eggs: Have ready

- a 3-quart saucepan
- 2 tablespoons white vinegar
- the 8 fresh eggs
- a custard or coffee cup
- a wooden spoon or spatula
- a large, slotted spoon
- a bowl large enough to hold the 8 poached eggs, filled ¾ with warm (not boiling) water

Fill the saucepan with cold water to a depth of about 2½ inches. Add vinegar and bring water to a rolling boil, then lower heat so water is simmering.

Break one egg into a custard or coffee cup. Using the wooden spoon, swirl the simmering water, then gently slide egg into water. With wooden spoon, immediately lift the white around the yolk. (Don't worry if a bit of the white floats off. Most will wrap around the egg.)

Break remaining eggs, one by one, into the cup and continue the procedure as with the first egg.

Permit each egg to poach from 3 to 4 minutes. Then using the slotted spoon, transfer poached eggs to the bowl of warm water.

Grilling the ham: Melt butter in a large skillet and grill ham slices over medium heat, turning each once, just until the slices become hot and glazed. Remove slices and drain on paper toweling.

Hollandaise Sauce

Makes about 1 cup

½ cup (1 stick) sweet butter
3 large egg yolks
2 to 2½ tablespoons fresh lemon juice

⅛ teaspoon salt
Pinch of cayenne pepper
1 to 2 tablespoons boiling water

Have all ingredients at room temperature before starting.

Use a double boiler or a 1-quart saucepan set over simmering, never boiling, water. Cut the butter into three equal parts.

Place 1 piece of butter in top of double boiler. Add the 3 yolks and beat with a whisk or wooden spoon until butter is completely melted.

Add the next 2 pieces of butter, one at a time, beating each until melted. Add lemon juice, salt and cayenne pepper, and continue to beat mixture until sauce thickens to the consistency of heavy cream. This will take from 10 to 12 minutes. Add a tablespoon or 2 of boiling water. Taste to correct seasoning. (You may like a bit more lemon juice or cayenne.)

If you do not plan to use the sauce immediately, cover the pot and keep the sauce warm over hot, not boiling, water. If the sauce becomes too thick, add 1 to 2 additional tablespoons of hot water and stir until smooth.

Huevos en Cazuela

Vary the amount of chilies according to your personal preference. Other sweet or hot chilies can be substituted for the poblano and jalapeño. Always use caution when working with chilies as their oils can burn the skin. Be sure to wash your hands thoroughly after handling the peppers.

4 servings

2 poblano chilies*
2 jalapeño chilies*

3 tablespoons unsalted butter
1 medium onion, sliced
⅛ teaspoon minced garlic (optional)
1 large tomato, peeled, cored, seeded, juiced and chopped
3 to 4 tablespoons minced ham

Salt and freshly ground pepper

8 eggs, room temperature
Salt and freshly ground pepper
4 to 6 ounces Monterey Jack cheese, Teleme or queso fresco, grated or minced
1 dozen warm tortillas (preferably homemade)

Preheat broiler. Generously butter four 2-cup soufflé or other baking dishes and set aside. Arrange poblano and jalapeño chilies on broiler pan and broil 3 inches from heat source, turning with tongs until charred on all sides, about 5 to 10 minutes. Transfer to plastic bag and seal tightly. Let steam about 10 minutes. Peel chilies and cut in half. Discard seeds, veins and cores. Rinse under cold water. Pat dry and cut into ⅛-inch julienne.

Melt butter in heavy large saucepan over medium heat. Add onion and garlic. Cover and cook until translucent, stirring occasionally, about 10 minutes. Add chilies and cook 5 minutes longer. Remove from heat and stir in tomato and ham. Cook until liquid is absorbed. Season with salt and pepper to taste. Using slotted spoon, divide onion mixture among prepared dishes. *(Can be prepared 1 day ahead to this point, covered and refrigerated.)*

To serve, preheat broiler. Warm dishes in broiler about 2 minutes. Break 2 eggs into each. Season with salt and pepper. Sprinkle with enough cheese to cover yolks completely. Broil eggs as close to heat source as possible until whites are firm and cheese has browned, about 3 to 5 minutes. (Eggs will continue cooking after removal from broiler.) Serve accompanied with tortillas and butter.

*If canned chilies are used, omit roasting.

🍒 *Poached and Boiled Eggs*

The seemingly simple operations of boiling and poaching eggs require a certain basic expertise if the result is to have the moist, golden yolk and tender white that characterize the perfectly cooked egg. Once the necessary techniques are mastered, however, poached and boiled eggs become a wonderful focus for breakfast and brunch—eggs Benedict is a special favorite.

Eggs that you plan to boil or poach should be at room temperature, but beyond that, the requirements differ. It is very important that eggs that are to be poached be fresh, but those intended for boiling should be about three days old. As they lose freshness they also lose the acidity that makes them so difficult to peel. But don't keep them much longer, or they will lose flavor.

Poached eggs have a French heritage. The name derives from the French term for pocket, referring to the fact that when the egg is broken into simmering water, the white forms a pocket enclosing the yolk. The procedure goes fast, so you may find it easier to poach only one or two eggs at a time unless you have individual metal egg poachers. Preheat well-buttered cups in simmering water, then break an egg directly into each.

To poach eggs: Fill a wide, nonaluminum skillet with water to a depth of 2 inches. Add ¼ cup of plain white vinegar (this helps to set the whites—colored vinegar stains the eggs, and wine vinegar contributes an undesirable flavor). Imagine that the skillet is a clock and point its handle to 12 o'clock. Bring the poaching liquid in the skillet to a rolling boil. Place a bowl filled with ice water next to the skillet. Crack an egg and position it crack side down at 12 o'clock. Holding the egg as close to the surface of the water as possible, open the shell just wide enough for the egg to slip into the water. With a slotted spoon, quickly turn the egg over until the white is wrapped around the yolk. If you like, immediately add a second egg at 3 o'clock, a third egg at 6 o'clock and a fourth egg at 9 o'clock (see figure). Reduce heat so water is barely bubbling. Simmer eggs 3 minutes (very large eggs may need 4) until whites are nicely set and yolks just feel resistant to the touch.

Poached Eggs and Creamed Chard

The Swiss chard can be prepared the day before serving and refrigerated overnight in the skillet, leaving the brunch cook little to do in the morning. Poached Eggs and Creamed Chard can also be served in warmed brioche.

6 servings

1 large bunch Swiss chard

Sauce
  2 tablespoons (¼ stick) butter
  2 tablespoons flour
  2 cups milk
  ½ cup whipping cream
  1 ounce freshly grated Emmenthaler or Parmesan cheese (¼ cup)
  1 tablespoon fresh lemon juice
  1 teaspoon salt
  ¼ teaspoon freshly ground pepper
  ⅛ teaspoon freshly grated nutmeg

Croutons
  6 ¼-inch-thick slices firm-textured white bread
  4 tablespoons clarified butter

  6 eggs
  Salt and freshly ground pepper

For chard: Cut leaves from stalks and set aside. Wash stalks; peel off fibers and dice stalks. Cook in large pot of rapidly boiling salted water until just tender, about 5 minutes. Refresh under cold water. Drain well and set aside.

Wash leaves, *do not dry,* and place in heavy skillet. Cover and cook initially

With a slotted spoon, remove eggs in the order in which they were placed in the pan and transfer to bowl of ice water.

To store and serve, trim uneven edges with a scissors or knife. If not serving immediately, cover with fresh cold water and refrigerate up to several days. To reheat, place eggs in a pan of salted water (1 teaspoon salt for each 3 cups of water) and heat just until water is too hot to touch. Remove eggs and pat dry with a towel.

Boiled eggs should not really be boiled, but simmered. Fill a heavy non-aluminum saucepan with enough cold water to cover eggs completely. Place eggs in saucepan. Bring to a boil over medium-high heat, then reduce heat so water is barely bubbling. Cook 3 minutes for soft; 15 minutes for hard. Overcooking discolors the yolks. Run under cold water until cool. To peel, tap the shell all over with a knife handle, rub egg between hands and start peeling at the broad end. Wash off any clinging bits of shell. Pat dry and use immediately, or store in the refrigerator several days. Unpeeled eggs keep several weeks.

Great Hints

- Many boiled and poached egg entrées can be completely assembled a day or so in advance. Combine eggs with other ingredients, cover with a sauce or aspic and refrigerate. Those that are to be served hot can be baked for 5 minutes in an oven preheated to 450°F or run under the broiler until golden brown.

- To avoid confusing cooked with uncooked eggs in the refrigerator, place outer skins of brown onions in the pot as eggs are cooking, to color the shells.

- Eggs can also be poached in white wine, beer, milk, cream, stock, tea or vegetable juice, or poached-fried in hot oil (cook 1 minute only with oil).

over medium-high heat, stirring occasionally, until leaves are tender, about 10 minutes; reduce heat near end of cooking time to prevent burning. Refresh under cold water. Squeeze out excess moisture; chop finely.

For sauce: Melt butter in 12-inch skillet. Whisk in flour and let foam 3 minutes over medium-high heat. Add milk and bring to boil. Reduce heat and simmer gently, stirring occasionally, until reduced almost by half, about 30 minutes. Strain and return to skillet. Add whipping cream, chard leaves and stalks. Simmer gently 10 to 15 minutes, stirring occasionally. Add cheese, lemon juice, salt, pepper, and nutmeg. Taste and adjust seasoning. *Cool and refrigerate if not using immediately.*

For croutons: Cut bread into large rounds using fluted cutter. Melt 2 tablespoons clarified butter in heavy large skillet over medium-low heat. Add 3 pieces of bread and sauté until lightly browned on both sides. Repeat with remaining butter and bread. Arrange on individual plates and keep warm.

For poached eggs: Bring sauce to gentle simmer in skillet. Form 6 "nests" in sauce using back of spoon. Break egg into each nest. Cover and cook until egg whites are just set, about 5 minutes. Season to taste with salt and pepper. Arrange eggs and chard on each crouton and serve immediately.

Tomato-Baked Eggs

6 servings

6 ripe medium to large tomatoes

2 tablespoons oil
3 tablespoons minced fresh parsley
3 garlic cloves, mashed
Salt

6 eggs
6 tablespoons grated Swiss cheese
6 tablespoons fine soft breadcrumbs
1 tablespoon butter, melted

Preheat oven to 375°F. Cut ½ inch off stem end of each tomato. Carefully scoop out most of pulp and seeds and set aside. Turn tomatoes upside down on paper towels to drain.

Heat oil in small frying pan over medium heat. Add parsley and garlic and sauté until soft. Divide mixture among tomatoes and sprinkle lightly with salt. Set in shallow baking dish just large enough to hold tomatoes. Carefully break egg into each and sprinkle with 1 tablespoon cheese. Combine breadcrumbs with butter and divide evenly over tops of tomatoes. Combine reserved tomato pulp with a little water in food processor or blender and puree. Pour into dish around tomatoes. Bake until eggs are set, about 12 to 15 minutes.

Trattoria Eggs

2 servings

¼ pound sweet or hot Italian
   sausage, casings removed
2 hard-cooked eggs, shelled
1 egg, beaten
Flour

Oil for deep frying
½ cup fine dry Italian or French
   breadcrumbs
¼ cup finely grated Parmesan cheese

Preheat oven to 400°F. Moisten work surface lightly with water. Divide sausage in half and pat each portion into a round on dampened surface. Lightly dip hard-cooked eggs in beaten egg, then roll in flour. Wrap each in sausage round, enclosing completely.

Heat oil to 370°F. Combine breadcrumbs and cheese in small bowl. Brush sausage-wrapped eggs with beaten egg. Roll eggs in breadcrumb mixture, coating well. Fry until breadcrumbs are golden brown and sausage is firm, about 2 to 3 minutes. Drain on paper towels. Transfer to baking dish and bake, uncovered, for 10 minutes. Let cool slightly. Drain on paper towels. Refrigerate until ready to serve.

Scrambled Eggs and Omelets

Kentucky Scrambled Eggs

4 servings

4 ounces cream cheese

4 tablespoons (½ stick) butter
½ cup chopped green bell pepper
½ cup chopped red bell pepper
½ cup chopped green onion
1 cup cooked corn, drained

6 eggs, lightly beaten
Salt and freshly ground pepper
Pinch of ground red pepper
Chopped green onion (garnish)
Crumbled cooked bacon (garnish)

Place cream cheese in top of double boiler and set over simmering water. Cook over low heat until cheese melts. Remove from heat and set aside.

Melt 2 tablespoons butter in large skillet over medium-high heat. Add bell peppers and green onion and sauté until onion is translucent, about 3 to 5 minutes. Blend into cream cheese. Stir in corn, mixing thoroughly.

Melt remaining 2 tablespoons butter in same skillet over medium-low heat. Add eggs and cream cheese mixture. Season to taste with salt, pepper, and red pepper. Cook, stirring occasionally, until eggs are barely set. Transfer to heated platter. Sprinkle with green onion and bacon. Serve immediately.

Classic Omelet

This omelet should take between 30 and 60 seconds to prepare.

1 or 2 servings

3 **large eggs**
½ **teaspoon salt**
⅛ **teaspoon freshly ground white pepper**
1 **teaspoon water**
1 **tablespoon unsalted butter**

1 **teaspoon unsalted butter**
⅛ **teaspoon freshly ground white pepper**
1 **teaspoon minced fresh parsley**

Slowly heat a 10-inch, curved-sided, nonstick skillet over low to moderate heat (this may take as long as 10 minutes). The pan must be sufficiently hot so that a dab of butter dropped into it sizzles, but does not brown. If pan overheats, cool for a few moments and reheat slowly until it is the correct temperature. Meanwhile, combine eggs, salt, pepper and water in a small bowl and beat with whisk. When pan reaches the correct temperature, add 1 tablespoon butter and, increasing heat to medium-high, tilt pan so that melting butter coats bottom. When butter stops foaming, add eggs all at once. Immediately begin to shake pan with one hand while simultaneously using the other hand to stir eggs in circular motion with the flat of a fork. At first, the fork should touch the bottom of the pan as you stir, so that eggs are moved all around the pan and away from the sides. As eggs begin to set, stir only the surface, always with a circular motion. When eggs are lightly set (omelet must be soft because it will continue to cook from its own interior heat after it has been removed from the pan) place filling or sauce down the center, if desired, and fold as shown in box, page 9. Spread 1 teaspoon butter on top and dust with pepper and parsley.

Omelet à la Lyonnaise

1 serving

2 **tablespoons (¼ stick) butter**
1 **large onion (about 8 ounces), thinly sliced**

2 **large eggs**
2 **tablespoons water**
½ **teaspoon salt**
Freshly ground white pepper

1 **to 2 tablespoons red wine vinegar**
1 **tablespoon butter**

Melt butter in small heavy skillet over low heat. Add onion and cook slowly until very soft, about 30 minutes, *but do not allow to brown.*

Combine eggs, water, salt and pepper in food processor or mixing bowl and blend well. Prepare Classic Omelet (see preceding recipe).

Turn omelet out onto warmed platter. Add vinegar and butter to onion mixture. When sizzling, pour over omelet and serve immediately.

🍎 Omelets

Contrary to popular opinion, there is no mystique involved in making an omelet. Novice cooks—and some veterans—often look with misgiving upon this versatile, delicious egg dish, suspecting that its creation demands special skills, like split-second timing and an agile wrist. Not so. What you need for a good omelet are reasonable instructions and a good pan.

Once mastered, the omelet becomes a standby for breakfast, brunch, lunch or dinner, for casual entertaining as well as for family meals. It is economical and easy to prepare—usually from ingredients on hand—and can be dressed up or down as the occasion demands. A simple, buttery omelet devoid of ornamentation can stand on its own at breakfast and, with the addition of an easy filling, can be the mainstay of a more elaborate brunch. More complicated seasonings and fillings convert the same omelet into an elegant entrée for a luncheon or light supper.

Omelets come in two basic styles: the classic French, firm on the outside but soft and creamy within, and the puffy variety, which has a soufflé-like texture. The difference between them is in the method of mixing and cooking: the yolks and whites are beaten together to make a classic version, and it is cooked over direct heat; for a puffy omelet the yolks and whites are beaten separately, then combined and baked.

Filling Suggestions
Sautéed chicken livers
Duxelles
Shrimp and mushrooms
Asparagus
Oysters and bacon
Tomatoes and eggplant
Grated Monterey Jack cheese and chopped green chilies
Red caviar with sour cream and dillweed
Sliced avocado, grated Monterey Jack cheese and alfalfa sprouts

Puffy Omelet

1 serving

3 large eggs, separated	1 tablespoon unsalted butter
1½ tablespoons flour	1 teaspoon freshly ground white pepper
⅛ teaspoon cream of tartar	1 teaspoon minced fresh parsley
⅛ teaspoon salt	

Preheat oven to 375°F. With electric mixer, set on medium speed, beat yolks until lemon colored. Add flour and beat until thoroughly blended.

In a separate bowl, beat egg whites until foamy. Add cream of tartar and salt and continue beating until stiff peaks form. Fold into yolk mixture.

Slowly heat a 10-inch nonstick ovenproof skillet. When a dab of butter sizzles in pan but does not brown, add 1 tablespoon butter and tilt pan so butter coats bottom and sides. Spread egg mixture over bottom and up sides of pan. Place pan in middle of oven and bake 11 minutes or until omelet is puffy and outside is slightly firm. Remove from oven, spread with filling if desired, and fold into thirds lengthwise. Turn onto a heated plate. Spread with 1 teaspoon butter and dust with white pepper and parsley.

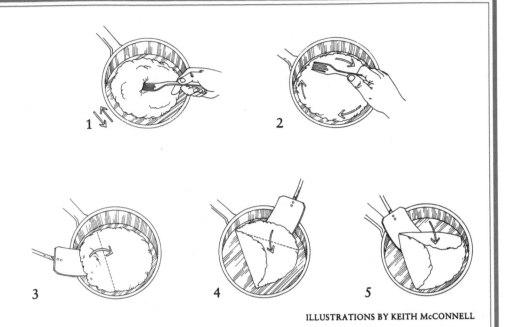

ILLUSTRATIONS BY KEITH McCONNELL

Great Hint

If making several omelets, beat the necessary number of eggs and the seasonings together in a bowl and use a ladle or measuring cup to pour out the right amount. Two large eggs measure about ⅓ cup; 3 eggs, ½ cup. *To fold an omelet, consider the omelet pan a clock, with the handle as 12 o'clock (see diagram). Tilt pan slightly. Place a pancake turner under the omelet at 10 o'clock. Lift omelet, and fold over toward center. Place the pancake turner under omelet at 2 o'clock and fold over again. With pan tilted, use pancake turner to loosen the omelet at 12 o'clock and fold it toward the center. With handle in the palm of one hand and a warm plate in the other hand at a right angle to the pan, roll the omelet onto the heated plate.*

Sprout Peanut Omelet

1 serving

> 2 eggs
> ¼ cup unsalted peanut halves, roasted
> 3 tablespoons minced green onion
>
> 1 teaspoon soy sauce
> ½ cup delicately flavored sprouts (cress, radish or alfalfa)
> 4 teaspoons peanut or safflower oil

Beat eggs in small bowl. Stir in peanuts, onion and soy sauce. Fold in sprouts. Heat oil in small skillet or omelet pan over medium heat. Add egg mixture and cook, pulling omelet away from sides as it sets. Fold once and continue cooking, turning once, until lightly golden on both sides. Serve hot.

French Scrambled Eggs

As Escoffier points out, these eggs cooked in a water bath take longer than if cooked over direct heat, but the water bath method guarantees a perfect result—the smooth and creamy texture that is the quality of this preparation. The consistency of the cooked eggs should be pourable but not runny, similar to very softly whipped cream.

A heavy pan is essential or the eggs will cook too quickly, becoming tough and grainy. Note, too, that this recipe is difficult to do in any smaller quantities.

4 servings

Bread Cases
1 12-inch sandwich-type loaf unsliced firm-textured white bread (2 days old)
Melted butter
1 garlic clove

Eggs
6 tablespoons (¾ stick) unsalted butter (cut 2 tablespoons into pieces and chill thoroughly to add at end of cooking)

8 eggs (extra large or jumbo)
Salt and freshly ground pepper
¼ cup whipping cream
60 asparagus tips,* briefly cooked in 2 tablespoons butter

For bread: Preheat oven to 325°F. Cut bread into 4 slices 1½ to 2 inches thick. Trim off all crust. Hollow out bread cases leaving base and walls about ½ inch thick. Coat inside and out with melted butter. Set on rack over baking sheet and bake, turning so all sides become golden brown, about 25 minutes. Remove from oven and gently rub outsides with garlic. *(Can be made an hour or so ahead and reheated briefly.)*

For eggs: Coat bottom and sides of top of double boiler with 2 tablespoons butter. Beat eggs just until mixed (do not overbeat or whisk). Add salt and pepper and 2 more tablespoons unchilled butter broken into pieces. Set pan over simmering water and stir eggs constantly with wooden spoon, making sure to scrape all surfaces of pan, especially corners, for about 10 minutes. If eggs start to thicken too quickly, remove pan from water for a minute or two. When eggs are nearly done (still quite loose), stir in cream and half of asparagus. Cook about a minute longer. Remove from heat and stir in chilled butter a piece at a time (this will stop cooking as well as enrich texture and flavor of eggs). Pour eggs into hot bread cases, letting some of mixture spill over sides. Garnish with remaining asparagus tips and serve immediately.

*Asparagus soup can be made from remaining asparagus stalks. Cover stalks with chicken broth or stock and cook until tender. Puree with some of the liquid. Pass through sieve to remove fibers. Add enough broth to achieve desired consistency and heat through. Enrich with a bit of cream and butter. Makes 2 or 3 servings.

Spanish Garden Omelet Loaf

Wrapped in layers of foil, this delicious combination of sturdy bread and flavorful eggs will keep warm up to 4 hours. Loaf can also be prepared ahead, wrapped in foil and chilled. Reheat about 25 minutes at 400°F. You might preview this dish with gazpacho.

6 servings

1 large round sourdough French or Italian bread (about 9½ to 12 inches)
4 tablespoons olive oil

1 onion, chopped
1 green pepper, chopped
1 garlic clove, minced or pressed

1½ to 2 cups lightly cooked mixed vegetables (peas, green beans, carrots, mushrooms, potatoes) and peeled, seeded and chopped raw tomatoes
Salt and freshly ground pepper
9 eggs, lightly beaten

Split bread horizontally and remove some of center from each side to form slight depression for omelet. Brush cut surfaces with 1 tablespoon olive oil. Reassemble loaf, wrap in foil and keep warm in 300°F oven.

For omelet: Heat remaining 3 tablespoons oil in nonstick or well-seasoned 10-inch skillet over medium-high heat. Add onion, green pepper and garlic and sauté until soft. Add mixed vegetables and salt and pepper to taste. Stir gently until heated through. Add eggs and cook over medium heat, shaking pan frequently and loosening edges of omelet so it does not stick, until center is almost set and underside has flecks of golden brown. Invert plate over skillet and flip omelet back onto it. Slide omelet into pan and cook until second side is browned, about 1 to 2 minutes.

Remove bread from oven and unwrap. Place bottom half cut side down on omelet and quickly flip pan over so omelet is on bread. Cover with top of loaf. Slice into wedges to serve.

Mixed Vegetable Terrine with Béchamel and Red Pepper Puree

A salad spinner seems to have been invented for this recipe, but if neither it nor a potato masher is available, give the vegetables a hard squeeze to rid them of excess liquid. This is excellent with chicken breasts.

Terrine can be assembled several days in advance and refrigerated before baking.

Recipe can be doubled and baked in 2 molds, or in 1 large mold (increase baking time to about 1½ hours).

Sauce can be further enriched with egg yolks.

8 servings

¾ to 1 pound mushrooms, coarsely chopped
3 cups milk

¾ pound cabbage (½ medium-size head)
2 large leeks (½ pound)
1 large bunch spinach
1 large bunch sorrel (optional)

Salt and freshly ground pepper

6 tablespoons (¾ stick) butter
6 tablespoons flour

1 tablespoon minced fresh tarragon or 1 teaspoon dried, crumbled
1 tablespoon minced fresh chervil or 1 teaspoon dried, crumbled

1 tablespoon minced chives or green onion
1½ to 2 teaspoons salt
1½ teaspoons minced fresh thyme or ½ teaspoon dried, crumbled
¼ teaspoon freshly ground pepper
¼ teaspoon freshly grated nutmeg
1 cup whipping cream

3 eggs
½ cup cream cheese, cut into chunks and brought to room temperature
Juice of 1 lemon

½ cup fresh breadcrumbs

1 medium red bell pepper

Combine mushrooms and milk in heavy saucepan. Cover and bring to boil. Reduce heat and simmer 3 minutes. Remove from heat and let steep, stirring occasionally, while other vegetables are being prepared.

Bring large pot of salted water to boil. Cut and clean the vegetables, placing them in separate bowls. Quarter and core cabbage, discarding any wilted leaves, and chop coarsely. Cut off roots and tough outer green leaves of leeks and discard. Slice leeks in half lengthwise and cut each half into ½-inch pieces. Wash thoroughly. Stem spinach and sorrel and wash thoroughly.

Cook cabbage in boiling water until just tender, about 8 minutes. Transfer to salad spinner using slotted spoon. Refresh under cold water and spin dry. Return to bowl and sprinkle with salt and pepper. Add leeks to pot and cook until just tender, about 5 minutes.

Transfer to salad spinner, refresh under cold water and spin dry. Return to bowl and sprinkle with salt and pepper. Cook spinach until completely wilted, about 3 minutes. Transfer to salad spinner, refresh under cold water and spin dry. Chop coarsely. Return to bowl and sprinkle with salt and pepper. Cook sorrel until completely wilted, about 1 minute. Transfer to salad spinner, refresh under cold water and spin dry. Chop coarsely. Sprinkle with salt and pepper and add to spinach.

Transfer mushrooms to salad spinner with slotted spoon and spin dry. Turn into separate bowl and sprinkle with salt and pepper. Add mushroom liquid from spinner to saucepan with milk.

Melt butter in heavy saucepan over low heat. Whisk in flour and let foam 3 minutes without coloring, stirring constantly. Whisk in milk mixture and stir over medium-high heat until sauce comes to boil. Reduce heat; simmer until reduced to 3 cups, about 15 minutes.

Season with tarragon, chervil, chives, salt, thyme, pepper and nutmeg. Pour slightly more than half the sauce into bowl and let cool slightly. Blend cream into remaining sauce; set aside.

Preheat oven to 400°F. Beat eggs, cream cheese and lemon juice into sauce in bowl. Divide among cabbage, leeks, spinach and mushrooms. Taste each vegetable and adjust seasoning.

Generously butter 1- to 2-quart charlotte mold or 9 × 5 inch loaf pan. Line with buttered waxed paper and sprinkle with breadcrumbs. Layer mold with spinach, leeks, mushrooms and cabbage. Bake until puffed and browned and knife inserted in center comes out clean, about 50 minutes. Let stand at room temperature for 5 minutes before unmolding onto heated serving platter. (Terrine will stay warm about 30 minutes in a turned-off oven with door ajar.)

While terrine is cooking, simmer reserved sauce until reduced by half. Strain and return to pan. Keep warm.

Roast pepper over direct gas flame or under broiler until completely browned, about 5 minutes, turning frequently. Let stand 5 minutes in tightly closed plastic bag. Peel pepper; discard stem and seeds. Puree in blender or processor. Add to reserved sauce. Taste and adjust seasoning. Spoon around unmolded terrine and serve immediately.

Spinach Turban

Turban can be assembled one day before serving and refrigerated. Brush top with melted butter and allow butter to firm before covering. Brush with butter before baking.

The assembled dish can also be frozen. Defrost overnight in refrigerator and bring to room temperature before baking. If baked directly from freezer, increase baking time about 30 minutes.

8 servings

2 tablespoons (¼ stick) unsalted butter
1 large onion, minced
1 bunch green onions including tops, chopped
2 pounds spinach, thoroughly washed, well drained and chopped or 2 10-ounce packages frozen chopped spinach, thawed and well drained
6 eggs, lightly beaten
½ pound feta cheese, rinsed and crumbled
8 ounces (½ pound) pot cheese or lightly creamed cottage cheese
2 tablespoons uncooked farina or ½ cup breadcrumbs

½ cup chopped fresh parsley
⅓ to ½ cup minced fresh dillweed
Salt and freshly ground pepper
Freshly grated nutmeg

1 pound phyllo pastry sheets
1 pound unsalted butter, melted
1 cup breadcrumbs

Minced fresh parsley (garnish)

Melt 2 tablespoons butter in large saucepan over medium heat. Add onions and sauté until transparent. Reduce heat to low, add spinach and cook, stirring occasionally, until moisture has evaporated. Remove from heat. Stir in eggs, cheese, farina or breadcrumbs, parsley and dill and blend thoroughly. Season with salt, pepper and nutmeg to taste. Set aside.

Grease a 3-quart ring mold or bundt pan. Unfold pastry and cut in half lengthwise; cover with waxed paper and damp towel. Remove 1 sheet of pastry and place on another sheet of waxed paper. Brush with melted butter and lay diagonally across prepared mold, allowing pastry to extend 1½ inches over sides of pan and center opening. Gently but firmly press pastry against sides of mold. Cover other side of mold in same fashion. Sprinkle with breadcrumbs.

Continue, using ½ to ¾ of remaining sheets, and working evenly around mold to ensure uniform layers. Brush each sheet with butter and sprinkle with breadcrumbs as you work.

Preheat oven to 350°F. Fill mold with spinach mixture. Cut out pastry covering center hole. Cut remaining sheets of phyllo into pieces and place over filling. Fold overhanging pastry back onto pastry pieces, brush with butter and sprinkle with thin layer of breadcrumbs. Place mold on baking sheet and bake 1½ hours, or until crisp and golden. Let set at least 5 but not more than 15 minutes before unmolding onto warmed serving platter. Dust with minced parsley and serve.

Frittata Di Zucchine (Italian Egg Pancake with Zucchini)

A frittata, unlike a French omelet, must cook slowly over low heat until well done, but should be neither tough nor dry.

6 servings

2 tablespoons imported olive oil
1 large garlic clove, peeled and quartered lengthwise
3 small zucchini, cut into slices ¼ inch thick
  Flour
2 tablespoons minced parsley
½ teaspoon salt
⅛ teaspoon freshly ground white pepper

2 tablespoons (¼ stick) unsalted butter
8 eggs, lightly beaten
1 teaspoon salt
⅛ teaspoon freshly ground white pepper

Heat oil in large skillet over medium-high heat. Add garlic and sauté 1 to 2 minutes. Discard garlic. Dredge zucchini lightly in flour, shaking off excess. Add to skillet, reduce heat to medium and stir-fry until golden, about 8 to 10 minutes. Drain as much oil from skillet as possible. Sprinkle zucchini with parsley, ½ teaspoon salt and ⅛ teaspoon freshly ground white pepper. Remove from heat.

Melt butter in heavy 10-inch skillet over high heat. Quickly combine eggs with remaining salt and pepper. As soon as butter foams (it should not color), pour in egg mixture. Reduce heat to low and add zucchini, distributing evenly.

Preheat broiler.

Fry frittata slowly over direct heat, loosening edges and tilting skillet so uncooked portion runs underneath and pricking top with fork to allow uncooked portion to seep to bottom. When all but very top is softly set, slide under broiler and brown lightly, about 15 to 20 seconds. Cut into wedges and serve hot, or cool to room temperature before serving as is frequently done in Italy.

Asparagus and Ham Timbale with Hollandaise Sauce

8 first-course servings or 4 to 6 main-course servings

1 cup half and half
⅔ cup fresh breadcrumbs (made from firm-textured white bread)

2 pounds asparagus, tough ends removed

2 tablespoons (¼ stick) unsalted butter
½ cup minced onion
¾ cup chopped ham

⅓ cup freshly grated Parmesan cheese
⅓ cup grated Gruyère cheese
5 eggs, beaten
  Pinch of freshly grated nutmeg
  Salt and freshly ground pepper

Hollandaise Sauce (see following recipe)

Combine half and half and breadcrumbs in large bowl and let soak.

Meanwhile, chop asparagus medium-fine in processor or by hand. Cook briefly in large amount of boiling salted water until just tender. Drain in colander, then gently press out any excess liquid using back of spoon.

Preheat oven to 350°F. Generously butter 2-quart charlotte mold. Melt 2 tablespoons butter in small skillet over medium heat. Add onion and sauté until limp. Add ham and sauté briefly to heat through. Mix into breadcrumb mixture along with cheeses and beaten eggs. Stir in asparagus. Season with nutmeg, salt and pepper. Turn into mold.

Cover mold with round of buttered waxed paper and set into large pan. Add enough boiling water to pan to come halfway up sides of mold. Bake until mixture is set and knife inserted in center comes out clean, about 1 hour. Remove mold from water and let stand 5 minutes. Discard waxed paper. Unmold timbale onto serving platter and serve with Hollandaise Sauce.

Hollandaise Sauce

3 egg yolks	2 tablespoons hot water
1 tablespoon fresh lemon juice	Salt
½ cup (1 stick) unsalted butter, melted and sizzling hot	

Whisk egg yolks until smooth in top of double boiler set over hot (not simmering) water. Add lemon juice. Whisking constantly, gradually add hot butter in slow steady stream, blending completely. Whisk in water. Season with salt and continue stirring 1 minute.

 Soufflés and Mousselines

Beer and Cheese Soufflé

While this won't rise to the ethereal heights of a traditional soufflé, it is light, puffy and very simple to make.

6 servings

¼ cup (½ stick) butter, room temperature	½ pound sharp cheddar cheese, grated
2 tablespoons Dijon mustard	½ cup chopped green onion
10 slices day-old, firm-textured white bread, crusts removed	½ cup beer
4 eggs, separated	Pinch of cream of tartar
¾ cup milk	Pinch of salt
Salt and freshly ground pepper	
½ pound cooked ham, cut into ½-inch cubes	

Position rack in lower third of oven and preheat to 350°F. Generously butter 1½-quart soufflé dish. Cream butter with mustard. Spread each slice of bread generously with mixture. Cut bread into 1-inch cubes. Beat egg yolks with milk, salt and pepper. Add bread cubes, ham, cheese and onion and toss lightly. Let stand at room temperature for about 15 minutes. Stir in beer.

Beat egg whites until foamy. Add cream of tartar and salt and continue beating until stiff. Fold about ¼ of whites into bread mixture quite thoroughly. Gently fold in remainder. Turn into soufflé dish and bake until puffed and golden brown, 30 to 40 minutes. Serve immediately.

Cauliflower-Watercress Soufflé with Tomato Cream Sauce

6 servings

1½ tablespoons butter, room
    temperature
2 tablespoons dry breadcrumbs,
    toasted
2 tablespoons grated Swiss cheese

1½ teaspoons coarse salt
1 small head cauliflower, separated
    into florets
1 large bunch watercress or 5
    ounces spinach leaves

5 tablespoons all purpose flour
1 cup cold milk
    Salt and freshly ground pepper
    Freshly grated nutmeg

5 egg yolks, lightly beaten
⅓ cup grated Swiss cheese
¼ cup crème fraîche

5 to 6 egg whites
¼ teaspoon salt
¼ teaspoon cream of tartar
    Boiling water
    Tomato Cream Sauce (see
    following recipe)

Preheat oven to 350°F. Prepare 1½-quart soufflé dish by coating with butter. Combine breadcrumbs and 2 tablespoons Swiss cheese and sprinkle bottom and sides of mold. Chill.

Bring 4 quarts water to boil with salt in Dutch oven. Add cauliflower and parboil 6 minutes. Add watercress and continue boiling until cauliflower is just tender, about 5 minutes. Drain and refresh under cold running water. Squeeze dry in towel. Transfer to food processor or blender and puree.

Sift flour into nonaluminum saucepan. Gradually stir in milk until mixture forms smooth paste. Blend in remaining milk. Season to taste with salt, pepper and nutmeg. Place over medium heat and simmer, stirring constantly, until sauce is smooth and thick. Transfer to large mixing bowl. Beat small amount of hot sauce into egg yolks. Blend back into remaining sauce. Stir in puree and remaining cheese. Gradually add crème fraîche and mix well. Season to taste.

Beat egg whites in large bowl until foamy. Add salt and cream of tartar and continue beating until whites are stiff but not dry. Stir ¼ of whites into cauliflower mixture to loosen. Carefully fold in remaining whites. Spoon into prepared mold. Set in larger pan and pour boiling water around mold to depth of 2½ inches. Bake until soufflé is lightly browned and has begun to pull away from sides of mold, about 75 minutes. Cool several minutes before inverting onto serving platter. Spoon some of Tomato Cream Sauce over top and pass remainder in sauceboat.

Tomato Cream Sauce

Makes about 2½ cups

2½ tablespoons butter
3 tablespoons all purpose flour
1½ cups milk
½ cup whipping cream

1 tablespoon tomato paste (about)
    Salt and freshly ground pepper
    Freshly grated nutmeg

Melt butter in small nonaluminum saucepan over medium heat. Add flour and stir constantly until smooth. Remove from heat and gradually stir in milk, beating vigorously to blend. Place over medium heat and continue stirring until sauce comes to boil. Blend in cream and small amount of tomato paste (*sauce should be pale rose; add more tomato paste if necessary*). Continue boiling 2 minutes, stirring constantly. Remove from heat, taste and season with salt, pepper and nutmeg. Keep warm.

Asparagus Yogurt Soufflé

2 servings

⅓ cup cooked chopped asparagus
⅓ cup plain yogurt
1 egg yolk
2 tablespoons freshly grated Parmesan cheese

1 tablespoon fresh parsley leaves
2 egg whites
1 tablespoon cornstarch
Pinch of salt

Preheat oven to 325°F. Butter two 2-cup soufflé dishes. Combine asparagus, yogurt, egg yolk, 1 tablespoon cheese and parsley in processor or blender and puree. Transfer to medium bowl. Beat egg whites in another bowl until foamy. Add cornstarch and salt and continue beating until whites are stiff and glossy. Stir ⅓ of whites into asparagus mixture to lighten. Gently but thoroughly fold in remaining whites. Spoon evenly into prepared molds. Sprinkle with remaining cheese. Bake until set, about 30 to 35 minutes.

Seafood Soufflé

2 servings

3 tablespoons butter
3 tablespoons flour
1 cup milk
3 egg yolks
1 7½-ounce can shrimp, tuna, salmon or crab, rinsed, well drained and broken up

1 tablespoon fresh lemon juice
2 tablespoons mayonnaise
2 tablespoons grated Swiss cheese

4 egg whites

Lightly butter a 1-quart soufflé dish; set aside. Preheat oven to 375°F.

Melt 3 tablespoons butter in small saucepan over medium-low heat. Reduce heat to low, stir in flour and cook 2 to 3 minutes without browning. Gradually add milk and stir until thickened. Remove from heat and add egg yolks one at a time, stirring well after each addition. Toss seafood with lemon juice to refresh. Fold in seafood, mayonnaise and cheese.

Beat egg whites separately until stiff but not dry. Gently fold into yolk mixture. Pour into soufflé dish and bake 30 to 40 minutes, until puffed and golden. Serve immediately.

Mousselines of Potato, Onion and Garlic

These molds can be assembled early on the day they are to be baked. Once baked, they will stay warm in the hot water bath for 30 minutes.

4 servings

2½ quarts water
Salt
1 pound boiling potatoes, peeled and quartered
1 head garlic, unpeeled and separated into cloves
¼ cup (½ stick) butter, room temperature
¼ cup whipping cream
¾ teaspoon salt
¼ teaspoon freshly ground pepper
⅛ teaspoon freshly grated nutmeg

2 tablespoons (¼ stick) butter
1 small onion, minced
1 egg, room temperature
1 egg yolk, room temperature

Bring water to boil with salt in Dutch oven or large saucepan. Add potatoes and garlic and cook until tender. Drain. Push potatoes through fine sieve with mallet, pressing with straight up and down motion to prevent their becoming glutinous. Rub garlic through sieve. Transfer to bowl. Stir ¼ cup butter, cream, salt, pepper and nutmeg into potato-garlic mixture.

Melt remaining butter in heavy small skillet over low heat. Add onion, cover and cook, stirring occasionally, until tender, about 15 minutes. Transfer to processor or blender. Add egg and egg yolk and mix until almost pureed, stopping machine as necessary to scrape down sides of container. Sieve into potato mixture and blend thoroughly.

Preheat oven to 350°F. Generously butter four ½-cup molds; line with buttered parchment or waxed paper. Divide potato mixture among molds. Place in baking dish and pour in enough water to come ¾ up sides of molds. Bring to simmer over direct heat. Bake until mousselines just start to shrink around edge of molds and skewer inserted in centers comes out clean, about 45 minutes. Remove from water bath and let rest 10 minutes before unmolding. Run knife around edge of molds and turn out onto plates.

Diamond Jim's Oyster and Spinach Soufflé

Oysters and spinach can be cooked the day before the brunch and the soufflé base prepared early in the morning. Place a piece of plastic wrap directly on base to prevent crust from forming.

4 servings

Oysters

1½ cups whipping cream
20 small fresh oysters, shucked or 1 10-ounce jar fresh oysters, drained (liquor reserved)

⅔ cup milk

Spinach

1 large bunch spinach, stemmed, washed and lightly shaken
1 tablespoon butter
¼ cup whipping cream
2 teaspoons fresh lemon juice
Salt and freshly ground pepper
Freshly grated nutmeg

4 thin slices French bread, trimmed into 3-inch rounds and toasted

2¼ teaspoons each minced fresh tarragon and chervil or ¾ teaspoon each dried, crumbled

Soufflé

2 tablespoons (¼ stick) butter
2 tablespoons all purpose flour
3 egg yolks, room temperature
1 tablespoon fresh lemon juice
1 teaspoon grated lemon peel
3 tablespoons freshly grated Emmenthaler, Italian Fontina or Parmesan cheese
Salt and freshly ground pepper
Freshly grated nutmeg

3 egg whites, room temperature
Pinch of salt
Pinch of cream of tartar

1 tablespoon butter
1½ teaspoons fresh lemon juice
1 tablespoon minced fresh chives (garnish)

For oysters: Combine whipping cream and any oyster liquor in medium saucepan and bring to boil over medium-high heat. Remove from heat and add 10 oysters. Let stand at room temperature for 1 hour.

Meanwhile, pour milk into medium saucepan and bring to boil over medium-high heat. Remove from heat and add remaining 10 oysters. Let stand at room temperature for 1 hour.

For spinach: Stir spinach in heavy large skillet over medium-high heat until wilted and cooked, about 3 minutes. Let cool; squeeze dry and chop coarsely. Melt butter in same skillet over medium-high heat. Add spinach and cream and cook, stirring occasionally, until cream is absorbed, about 5 minutes. Remove from heat. Stir in lemon juice. Add salt, pepper and nutmeg.

Lightly butter 9 × 13-inch gratin or other baking pan. Arrange toast rounds in single layer in bottom of pan. Divide spinach mixture evenly over toast. Remove oysters from milk and cream using slotted spoon (reserving liquids) and mound atop spinach.

Blend tarragon and chervil into reserved cream. Place over medium-high heat and cook until sauce is reduced by half, about 30 minutes. Set aside.

For soufflé: Preheat oven to 400°F. Melt butter in heavy small saucepan over medium-low heat. Stir in flour and cook roux until bubbly (do not brown), 3 minutes. Increase heat to high, stir in reserved milk and bring to boil, stirring until very thick and smooth. Remove from heat. Blend in egg yolks, lemon juice, lemon peel and all but 2 teaspoons cheese. Add salt, pepper and nutmeg.

Combine egg whites, salt and cream of tartar in large mixing bowl and beat until whites are stiff and glossy. Gently fold ¼ of whites into yolk mixture to loosen, then fold yolks back into remaining whites. Spoon soufflé over oysters, covering completely. Sprinkle evenly with reserved cheese. Reduce oven temperature to 375°F. Bake soufflés until puffed and golden brown, about 15 minutes.

Meanwhile, slowly warm tarragon-cream sauce over low heat. Whisk in butter and lemon juice. Spoon sauce over soufflés, top with chives and serve.

Sweet Potato Soufflé

Sweet potatoes are also eaten for dessert in many Latin American countries. This soufflé can be prepared several hours ahead to point of adding egg whites. Store covered at room temperature.

4 to 6 servings

2 pounds sweet potatoes or yams

Vegetable oil

1 cup sour cream
2 tablespoons Marsala (or 1 tablespoon honey mixed with 1 tablespoon warm water)
¼ cup vegetable oil (preferably cold-pressed safflower)
1 tablespoon finely grated lemon peel

½ teaspoon sea salt or 1 teaspoon coarse salt
¼ teaspoon freshly grated nutmeg
4 egg yolks
5 egg whites

Mousseline Sauce (see following recipe)

Cook potatoes in enough boiling salted water to cover until tender, about 30 to 40 minutes (or bake in 375°F oven for 40 to 45 minutes). Let cool completely; peel. Press through strainer or food mill. Measure 2 cups puree.

Preheat oven to 400°F. Coat 1-quart soufflé dish with vegetable oil. Prepare foil collar and oil lightly; secure to dish with string or pins and set aside.

Beat puree, sour cream and Marsala in large bowl. Add ¼ cup oil, lemon peel, salt and nutmeg and mix well. Whisk in egg yolks. Beat egg whites in another large bowl until soft peaks form. Gently fold into potato mixture.

Spoon mixture into prepared dish. Place dish in oven and immediately reduce oven temperature to 375°F. Bake until soufflé is puffed and brown, about 35 minutes. Discard collar. Serve immediately. Pass sauce separately.

Mousseline Sauce

For sabayon-type sauce, omit cream.

Makes about 1½ cups

3 egg yolks
1 egg
¼ cup honey
2 tablespoons Sherry, Madeira or Marsala or 1 teaspoon lemon, vanilla, orange or almond extract

⅓ cup whipping cream, whipped

Combine yolks, egg, honey and wine in top of double boiler set over gently simmering water and whisk (or use rotary beater) until mixture holds its shape. Remove from heat. Fold in whipped cream, blending well.

Marmalade Soufflé

6 servings

Butter and granulated sugar
6 egg whites
6 tablespoons powdered sugar
Finely grated peel of 1 orange
8 ounces imported orange marmalade

Warmed orange marmalade (garnish)
Whipped cream and coarsely chopped toasted almonds (garnish)

Generously butter tops of two 1½-quart double boilers. Dust heavily with granulated sugar. Beat egg whites until soft peaks form. Add powdered sugar 1 tablespoon at a time and continue beating until very stiff. Fold in orange peel. Stir about ¼ of whites into marmalade. Gently fold in remainder. Divide between double boilers and set over simmering water. Cover and cook until soufflés are set, about 70 minutes.

Carefully invert onto heated serving platter(s) and place dollop of marmalade on top of each soufflé. Serve immediately with cream and almonds.

Whipped cream can be lightly flavored with orange liqueur if desired. Platter can also be garnished with baked orange sections that have been marinated in orange liqueur.

Quiches and Tarts

Baked Egg Custard with Onion and Bacon

This custard is also wonderful prepared quiche-style in a baked crust.

6 servings

3 tablespoons butter
2 large Spanish onions (1 pound total), thinly sliced
1½ ounces slab bacon (tough rind removed), cut julienne
6 eggs

1 cup whipping cream
¼ cup milk
1 teaspoon salt
½ teaspoon freshly grated nutmeg
Freshly ground white pepper

Generously butter shallow 4½-cup ovenproof dish. About 15 minutes before baking, position rack in center of oven and preheat to 300°F.

Melt butter in small saucepan over medium heat. Add onion, cover with circle of waxed paper and cook 10 minutes. Discard paper, reduce heat to medium-low and cook onion until completely soft but not brown, about 20 minutes, shaking pan occasionally.

Meanwhile, sauté bacon until cooked through but not crisp. Drain well on paper towels. Beat eggs in large bowl. Add onion, bacon and remaining ingredients and combine thoroughly, *but do not overmix*. Taste and adjust seasoning.

Ladle mixture into prepared dish. Bake until custard is browned and puffy, about 55 to 60 minutes. Let stand for about 10 minutes before cutting.

Fantasy Quiche

Creamy Mushroom Filling may be prepared up to 2 hours before using in quiche.

6 to 8 servings

3 tablespoons butter, room temperature
⅔ to 1 cup breadcrumbs, toasted
  Creamy Mushroom Filling (see following recipe)
8 ounces cream cheese, room temperature or 1 cup cottage cheese
1¼ cups crème fraîche or whipping cream
3 eggs

2 tablespoons minced fresh parsley or tarragon, or combination
1½ teaspoons dried thyme or oregano, or combination
  Salt and freshly ground pepper
  Freshly grated nutmeg
  Paprika

1 tablespoon oil
1 egg, beaten with salt to taste
5 ounces lean boiled ham, diced

Prepare 10½-inch quiche pan (preferably porcelain) by coating with butter and sprinkling bottom and sides with breadcrumbs. Refrigerate to set.

Prepare Creamy Mushroom Filling. Cover and set aside. Preheat broiler.

Combine cream cheese, ¾ cup crème fraîche, eggs, herbs and seasonings in food processor and blend well.

Heat oil in 8-inch omelet pan with ovenproof handle over medium heat. Add egg and tilt pan to coat entire bottom. When bottom is browned, run pan under broiler to brown top. Turn oven temperature to 350°F. Gently slide omelet into quiche pan. Spread evenly with mushroom filling and sprinkle with diced ham. Pour cream cheese mixture over top. Bake 35 to 40 minutes. *Quiche may be made a day or two ahead and refrigerated at this point.*

Twenty minutes before serving, pour remaining crème fraîche over top of quiche. Bake at 350°F until crème is set, about 10 to 15 minutes.

*For "instant" crème fraîche, add ¼ cup yogurt to 1 cup whipping cream.

Creamy Mushroom Filling

2 pounds mushrooms, sliced
1 tablespoon fresh lemon juice
2 tablespoons oil

1 cup half and half or evaporated milk or milk

Sprinkle mushrooms with lemon juice. Heat oil in large skillet over medium-high heat. Add mushrooms and sauté until heated through, about 3 minutes. Reduce heat, cover with half and half and simmer until liquid has almost evaporated and mushrooms are very lightly colored, about 15 to 20 minutes.

Spinach and Bacon Tart

6 to 8 servings

6 slices bacon, diced
2 tablespoons (¼ stick) butter
½ cup chopped onion

1½ to 2 pounds fresh spinach, cooked, drained, cooled and squeezed dry
3 tablespoons sour cream

1½ teaspoons dried dillweed
2 eggs
¼ pound feta cheese, crumbled

½ pound puff pastry dough or 4 frozen puff pastry shells
2 tablespoons (¼ stick) butter, melted

Sauté bacon until crisp. Drain on paper towels. Melt 2 tablespoons butter in small skillet over medium-high heat. Add onion and sauté until golden.

Combine spinach, onion, sour cream, dillweed and eggs in processor or blender and puree. Transfer to bowl and stir in bacon and feta cheese.

Preheat oven to 300°F. Grease 8-inch round baking dish. Divide puff pastry into 4 equal parts and roll each into 8-inch round. Reserve pastry scraps. Set 1 pastry round in bottom of prepared dish. Brush with some of melted butter. Top with another pastry round. Spread spinach mixture to within 1 inch of edges on all sides. Paint pastry rim with water. Top with another pastry round, brush with butter and add final pastry layer. Press edges of pastry together. Roll out pastry scraps and cut into decorations: leaves, flowers, etc. Brush with melted butter and bake until golden, about 45 to 50 minutes.

Tart of Leeks, Ham and Tomato

8 to 12 servings

Pastry
¾ cup (1½ sticks) chilled unsalted butter, cut into 6 pieces
1 egg
2 tablespoons cold water
½ teaspoon freshly grated nutmeg
Pinch of salt
1¾ cups unbleached all purpose flour (9½ ounces)

Filling
6 tablespoons (¾ stick) unsalted butter
4 large leeks (white part only), finely chopped

¾ cup finely diced ham
1 teaspoon salt
¼ to ½ teaspoon freshly grated nutmeg
Freshly ground pepper
6 eggs
1¼ cups whipping cream
Pinch of cayenne pepper

1 small tomato, peeled, seeded, juiced and diced
2 tablespoons minced fresh parsley

For pastry: Combine butter, egg, water, nutmeg and salt. Add flour and mix only until pastry begins to form a ball. Place in a plastic bag, press into a circle about 8 inches in diameter and chill at least 2 hours, preferably overnight.

Roll out dough on lightly floured board to thickness of ⅛ inch. Press into bottom and sides of 11- to 12-inch quiche pan with removable bottom. Using kitchen shears, trim dough 1 inch beyond pan. Fold this dough back inside to form a double thickness and press firmly. Prick bottom and sides with fork. Chill 30 minutes or until firm.

Preheat oven to 400°F. Melt butter in large skillet over medium heat. Add leeks, cover with circle of waxed paper and cook until leeks soften, about 10 to 15 minutes. Discard paper. Add ham to skillet and cook uncovered 2 minutes. Add salt, nutmeg and pepper and blend well. Remove from heat. Whisk eggs in large mixing bowl until foamy. Add cream, cayenne and leek mixture and blend thoroughly. Set aside.

Line quiche shell with parchment paper. Fill with dried beans or rice and bake 12 minutes. Remove paper and beans. Prick bottom and sides of crust again and bake until lightly browned, about 12 minutes. Remove from oven and reduce temperature to 325°F.

Ladle filling into hot crust to within ⅛ inch from top edge; *do not overfill*. Sprinkle with tomato and parsley. Bake until top is browned and puffy, about 40 minutes. Cool on wire rack 10 minutes before slicing and serving.

🍒 *Pastry Primer*

For a perfect pie crust every time, follow these four steps in order.

1. Combine dry ingredients. When using a food processor, remember that most machines can hold no more than 2½ to 3 cups of dry ingredients at one time.

2. Chill butter or other solid shortening. Cut into small pieces and mix with dry ingredients, using either food processor or pastry blender. Finished mixture should resemble coarse cornmeal. If when using pastry blender, shortening begins to melt, stop and place bowl and utensil in refrigerator for about 20 minutes before continuing.

3. Add liquid by tossing with a fork or mixing with food processor. If using fork, mix only until dough is just moistened and can be gathered into a loose ball. For processor, run machine until dough just begins to gather together. Overmixing will produce undesirable elasticity.

4. Let dough rest. Wrap it and chill anywhere from 30 minutes to overnight to ensure a tender crust. (After its initial rest, dough can be wrapped in an airtight package and frozen for up to 3 months.)

Flavoring

Any pastry dough may be flavored to taste by adding herbs, spices, ground nuts or other flours to the dry ingredients. Be generous with herbs and spices; they fade in baking.

Shortness

This is determined by the proportion of shortening to dry ingredients. A short dough results in a flaky, tender crust, and if butter is used, its inimitable overtones will come through. If too short, dough will actually melt away as it bakes. For deep-dish pies, we recommend a moderately short dough that will maintain its consistency during baking. Vary this to taste, but don't use more than 3 ounces (6 tablespoons) of shortening per cup of flour.

Mediterranean Tart

Can be assembled and baked ahead. Brush again with butter when reheating.

6 to 8 servings

3 tablespoons unsalted butter
1 onion, finely chopped
1 cup sliced mushrooms
¼ teaspoon dried thyme
2 tablespoons flour
1 cup chicken broth
2 tomatoes, peeled, seeded and chopped
1 whole chicken breast, poached, skinned, boned and cubed
¼ pound cooked ham, cubed
½ cup chopped pitted black olives, rinsed and drained

½ teaspoon anchovy paste
Freshly ground pepper
Salt

¾ cup (1½ sticks) unsalted butter, melted
16 sheets (about 16 × 12 inches) phyllo dough (½ pound)

½ cup freshly grated Parmesan cheese

Melt butter in large skillet over medium heat. Add onion and sauté until soft and translucent. Add mushrooms and thyme and cook about 5 minutes. Blend in flour and cook 2 to 3 minutes, stirring frequently. Add chicken broth and tomatoes and cook, stirring constantly, until thickened. Reduce heat, add chicken, ham, olives and anchovy paste and simmer gently 5 minutes. Season with pepper, and salt if necessary. Remove from heat and let cool.

Preheat oven to 300°F. Brush bottom and sides of 12×7×2-inch baking dish with some melted butter. Line dish with 1 sheet of phyllo, pressing firmly into corners and against sides of dish. Brush with melted butter, being sure to reach into corners and sides. Repeat until 8 sheets of phyllo are in dish.

Spoon filling over phyllo, spreading into corners. Sprinkle with all of cheese. Top with sheet of phyllo and brush with butter. Repeat with remaining phyllo. Trim excess from edges of dish using scissors. Brush top with some of remaining butter. Bake, brushing with butter several times, until pastry is crisp and golden, about 1 hour. Cut into squares while warm.

Deep-Dish Chili-Cheese Pie

Can be assembled and then refrigerated overnight. Bring to room temperature before baking.

10 to 12 servings

¼ cup oil
1 teaspoon minced fresh ginger root
7 mild long green chilies,* seeded, deveined and chopped
1 large onion, chopped
1 large garlic clove, minced
1 15-ounce can garbanzo beans, rinsed and drained
1½ teaspoons ground coriander or cilantro
1 teaspoon whole leaf oregano
¼ teaspoon cumin
¼ teaspoon cayenne pepper
1 cup pitted black olives, chopped
1 4-ounce jar or can pimiento, drained and chopped

Salt and freshly ground pepper
½ pound small fresh or frozen corn kernels
1 pound sharp cheddar cheese, shredded

1½ cups milk
3 eggs
½ teaspoon salt
⅛ teaspoon freshly ground pepper
Pinch of cayenne pepper
Pinch of ground coriander or cilantro

Cornmeal-Chive Pastry (see following recipe)

Heat oil in large wok or 14-inch skillet over high heat. Add ginger and stir-fry 30 seconds. Add chilies, onion and garlic and stir-fry 2 to 3 minutes. Add garbanzo beans, coriander, oregano, cumin and cayenne and stir-fry another minute. Remove from heat and add olives, pimiento, salt and pepper. Cool slightly. Stir in corn and set aside to cool completely. Drain if necessary, then stir in shredded cheese.

Position rack in center of oven and preheat to 350°F. Butter shallow 2½-quart baking dish. Combine milk, eggs, salt, pepper, cayenne and coriander and beat well. Spoon vegetable mixture in dish and pour custard over top.

Roll out pastry on floured surface to thickness of about ⅛ inch. Place over filling. Trim edges and press pastry to inside of dish to seal. Cut several slits in top to vent steam. Use scraps of dough to decorate crust, if desired. Bake until knife inserted in center comes out clean, about 1 to 1½ hours. Serve either hot or at room temperature.

*Always use caution when working with chilies as their oils can burn the skin. Be sure to wash your hands thoroughly after handling the peppers. If you want more of the chilies' natural hotness to come through, do not seed or devein; just discard stem and chop the entire pepper as fine as desired.

Cornmeal-Chive Pastry

Makes pastry for 1 pie

1½ cups unbleached all purpose flour
⅔ cup yellow cornmeal
¼ cup cake flour
½ teaspoon salt
3 tablespoons minced chives or green onion tops

½ cup plus 2 tablespoons (1¼ sticks) cold unsalted butter
½ cup (about) cold water

Follow four basic steps in Pastry Primer (see box, page 22).

Tourte of Sausage and Winter Fruits

Can be prepared 1 day ahead and reheated before serving.

6 to 8 servings

½ cup water
½ cup sour cream
2 tablespoons (¼ stick) unsalted butter
2 teaspoons sugar
2 teaspoons dry yeast

1 egg
1 teaspoon salt
½ teaspoon freshly ground white pepper
4 cups unbleached all purpose flour (16 ounces)

1 12-ounce package mixed dried pitted fruit, finely chopped

1 cup dry white wine

1 tablespoon butter
1 large onion, chopped
2 tablespoons Cognac
2 Granny Smith or Newtown apples, cored and finely chopped
1 pound kielbasa sausage, cooked, skinned and coarsely chopped
12 ounces Gruyère cheese, shredded
Salt and freshly ground pepper

1 egg beaten with 1 teaspoon cold water

Grease large bowl and set aside. Combine water, sour cream, butter and sugar in small saucepan over low heat and warm to 100°F. Remove from heat and let cool to about 60°F. Stir in yeast. Let stand until bubbly and proofed, about 10 minutes.

Transfer yeast mixture to processor. Add egg, salt and pepper and mix until blended. Mix in enough flour to make soft, slightly sticky dough. Continue mixing until dough is smooth and elastic. Transfer to prepared bowl, turning to coat entire surface. Cover and let stand at room temperature until more than doubled, about 1½ hours. Punch dough down and let rise again.

Meanwhile, combine mixed fruit and wine in medium bowl and set aside.

Melt butter in large skillet over medium-high heat. Add onion and sauté until browned. Drain wine from fruit and pour into skillet. Increase heat to high, add Cognac and boil, stirring constantly, until reduced to thin glaze. Remove from heat and stir in fruit, apples and sausage. Let cool. Blend in Gruyère. Season with salt and pepper.

Generously grease 11 × 1-inch tart pan with removable bottom. Punch dough down and transfer to lightly floured work surface. Remove ⅔ of dough and roll into 15-inch circle. Press circle into bottom of prepared pan, leaving generous overhang. Spoon fruit filling into pan. Roll out remaining dough as thinly as possible and trim to 13-inch circle (reserve scraps). Moisten edges of both pieces of dough with water. Arrange 13-inch circle over tourte, pinching edges to seal. Fold edges under to form thick coil of dough around tourte. Cut remaining scraps into long, thin strips and decorate top of tourte in crisscross pattern. Cover with towel and let rise until doubled, 1 hour.

Position rack in bottom third of oven and preheat to 375°F. Brush tourte with beaten egg. Bake until golden brown, about 50 minutes. Cool 20 minutes in pan; then carefully unmold onto wire rack. Serve warm.

Spiced Spinach Pie; Snow Pea and White Corn Salad

*Chicken Breasts Wrapped in Endive
with Herb Butter and Sauce Chivry;
Poached Eggs and Creamed Chard;
Cornets with Béchamel and Goat Cheese Filling*

Irwin Horowitz

Sliced Cucumber with Sour Cream;
Gravlax with Sweet Mustard Sauce

Seafood Strudel

*Flauta Tart (top); Tomato and Sausage Tart (center);
Spinach and Bacon Tart (foreground)*

Mixed Vegetable Terrine with Béchamel

Tomato and Sausage Tart

4 to 6 servings

2 teaspoons Dijon mustard
1 unbaked 9-inch pastry shell

½ pound Italian sausage

2 to 3 medium tomatoes, peeled, cored and thickly sliced
½ teaspoon salt

¼ teaspoon freshly ground pepper
½ teaspoon dried basil
¼ cup minced fresh parsley

1½ cups shredded cheddar cheese
½ cup mayonnaise

Position rack in lower third of oven and preheat to 400°F. Spread mustard over pastry and bake 5 minutes. Cool.

Remove sausage from casings. Sauté in small skillet, crumbling with fork, until cooked through. Drain and let cool.

Sprinkle sausage over pastry. Cover with tomato slices and sprinkle with salt, pepper, basil and parsley.

Combine cheese and mayonnaise in small bowl and blend well. Spread over tomato slices, sealing completely to edges. Bake until hot and bubbly, about 35 minutes. Serve immediately.

Flauta Tart

6 servings

1 unbaked 9-inch pastry shell or 1 12-inch flour tortilla
1 egg white, lightly beaten or oil

1 tablespoon oil
1 pound boneless lean beef
1½ teaspoons paprika
¼ teaspoon chili powder
1 large onion, chopped
1 large garlic clove, minced

1½ cups grated Monterey Jack cheese
1 cup sour cream

¾ cup chopped green onion
¼ cup coarsely chopped green chilies
3 eggs, beaten
1 teaspoon salt
¼ teaspoon freshly ground pepper
Sour cream and sliced avocado (garnish)
Salsa (optional)

Preheat oven to 400°F. If using pastry, fit into 9-inch tart or pie pan. Brush with egg white and bake 5 minutes. Let cool. If using tortilla, grease 9-inch pie pan, add tortilla and brush lightly with oil. Bake until top is very lightly browned, about 5 minutes.

Heat oil in large skillet over medium-high heat. Pat meat with mixture of paprika and chili powder. Add meat, onion and garlic to skillet and brown well. Reduce heat, cover partially and braise (do not add liquid) until tender, about 1 to 1½ hours. (If meat begins to stick, cover pan completely.) If liquid has accumulated when meat is tender, remove lid and cook until moisture has evaporated. Let meat cool, then shred coarsely using fingers or fork.

Preheat oven to 325°F. Combine meat, cooked onion and garlic, cheese, 1 cup sour cream, green onion, chilies, eggs, salt and pepper in large bowl and mix well. Turn into prepared pastry, spreading evenly. Bake 55 to 60 minutes, or until filling is set and crust is nicely browned. Cool slightly, then spread top with sour cream and decorate with avocado slices. Serve with salsa.

Salmon Pie

4 to 6 servings

1 11-ounce package pie crust sticks
2 eggs
½ cup milk
¼ cup chopped onion
2 tablespoons minced fresh parsley
1 tablespoon melted butter

¾ teaspoon dried basil, crumbled
¼ teaspoon salt
1 15½-ounce can salmon, drained (skin and bones removed)
Chilled Cucumber Sauce (see following recipe)

Preheat oven to 425°F. Grease 8-inch pie plate. Prepare 1 pie crust according to package directions. Roll dough out ⅛ inch thick. Trim into 9-inch circle. Slice into 8 wedges and set aside.

Beat eggs in medium bowl until light and fluffy. Add milk, onion, parsley, butter, basil and salt and mix well. Stir in salmon. Turn mixture into pie plate. Arrange pastry wedges over top, crimping edges to seal. Bake until top is golden brown, about 25 minutes. Serve with cucumber sauce.

Chilled Cucumber Sauce

Makes about 1 cup

½ cup sour cream
¼ cup mayonnaise
¼ cup grated onion
1 medium cucumber, peeled, halved lengthwise, seeded, grated and well drained

1 tablespoon minced fresh parsley
2 teaspoons vinegar

Combine all ingredients in small bowl and mix well. Cover and refrigerate until ready to use.

Spanakopitta (Spinach, Onion and Cheese Pie)

This delicious dish can be prepared up to 8 hours ahead and refrigerated (do not freeze). Reheat in 325°F oven until warmed through, 35 minutes.

8 to 10 servings

3 bunches spinach, washed, drained and finely chopped (about 2 pounds)
10 green onions, chopped
½ cup chopped fresh parsley
6 eggs
1¼ pounds feta cheese, rinsed and crumbled
½ pound ricotta or farmer's cheese
½ cup freshly grated Kefalotyri or Parmesan cheese

2 tablespoons milk
1 tablespoon dried oregano, crumbled
Freshly ground pepper

24 thin phyllo pastry sheets (about 1 pound)
1 cup (2 sticks) unsalted butter, melted with ½ cup olive oil

Sesame seed

Combine spinach, onion and parsley in large bowl and toss to mix well. Beat eggs in medium bowl with fork. Add cheeses, milk, oregano and pepper and beat well. Taste and adjust flavoring (add more ricotta if too strong, more Kefalotyri if too bland). Blend cheese mixture into spinach.

Preheat oven to 375°F. Generously butter 9 × 13 × 2-inch baking pan. Reserve 8 phyllo sheets for top layer (cover with waxed paper and damp towel to prevent drying). Generously brush each remaining phyllo sheet with butter and stack in pan, turning slightly so corners fan out around pan.

Pour spinach mixture over phyllo, smoothing with spatula. Fold excess phyllo over filling 1 sheet at a time, brushing each with butter as you work. Brush each reserved sheet with melted butter and place over top, folding ends under as necessary to fit into pan. Brush top with butter and sprinkle evenly with sesame seed.

Make 5 to 6 slits through top of pastry with sharp knife to allow steam to escape. Bake until golden and crisp, about 50 minutes. Serve hot.

Crabmeat Tart

Makes one 10- or 11-inch tart or twelve 3½- to 4-inch tartlets

2 tablespoons dry whole wheat breadcrumbs
1 10- or 11-inch baked Whole Wheat Short Pastry shell (see following recipe)
1 tablespoon light vegetable oil (preferably cold-pressed safflower)
6 ounces firm mushrooms, thinly sliced
1 teaspoon fresh lemon juice
1 tablespoon chopped fresh dill or 1½ teaspoons dried dillweed
Herb or vegetable salt

1 to 1½ cups coarsely flaked crabmeat
1½ cups half and half or double-strength reconstituted nonfat dry milk, scalded
3 eggs
2 egg yolks
¼ cup (½ stick) unsalted butter, melted and cooled
6 tablespoons freshly grated Parmesan cheese
1 tablespoon finely chopped fresh parsley
Sweet paprika

Sprinkle breadcrumbs evenly over bottom of pastry shell and set aside.

Heat oil in medium skillet over medium-high heat. Add mushrooms and lemon juice and sauté until softened, about 1 to 2 minutes. Add dill and season with herb salt to taste. Remove from heat and stir in crabmeat.

Preheat oven to 350°F. Combine half and half, eggs, egg yolks, melted butter and 4 tablespoons Parmesan cheese in large bowl and whisk until blended. Add crabmeat mixture. Spoon into pastry shell. Bake until filling is set, about 35 to 40 minutes. Sprinkle with remaining Parmesan cheese and parsley. Dust lightly with paprika. Let cool 10 minutes before cutting into wedges.

Whole Wheat Short Pastry

Makes one 10- or 11-inch shell or 36 to 48 hors d'oeuvre-size tartlet shells. Will also make twelve 3½- to 4-inch tartlet shells.

2 cups whole wheat pastry flour
½ cup plus 2 tablespoons (1¼ sticks) cold unsalted butter, cut into ½-inch pieces
2 teaspoons fresh lemon juice

¼ to ⅓ cup ice water

Additional whole wheat pastry flour

Combine flour and butter in large bowl and blend with fingertips until mixture resembles coarse meal. Add lemon juice and ¼ cup ice water and blend well, working dough as little as possible and adding more water 1 tablespoon at a time if dough is too dry. Turn dough out onto unfloured work surface and quickly form into ball.

Cover with plastic; chill 30 minutes.

Cut 2 pieces of waxed paper 24 inches long. Place 1 sheet on work surface and dust with additional flour. Set dough in center of paper and sprinkle with flour. Flatten dough with rolling pin and cover with remaining paper.

Roll dough out to thickness of ⅛ inch. Remove top sheet of waxed paper. Lifting bottom sheet, invert dough into 10- or 11-inch tart pan. Press dough firmly against sides and bottom. Run rolling pin over rim to trim off excess dough. Prick bottom and sides with fork (if filling to be used is liquid, such as custard, do not prick through).

Preheat oven to 350°F. Line pastry with waxed paper and fill with dried beans or rice. Bake 25 minutes. Discard paper and beans or rice. Continue baking until bottom is browned, about 10 minutes. Let cool. Fill as desired.

For tartlet shells: Arrange tartlet tins on baking sheet with sides touching. After rolling dough between sheets of waxed paper, remove top sheet. Lifting bottom sheet, invert dough over tins. Press dough firmly against sides and bottoms. Run rolling pin over top to trim off excess dough. Prick bottoms with fork. Line pastries with waxed paper and fill with dried beans or rice. Bake in 350°F oven 10 to 15 minutes, depending on size of tins. Discard paper and beans or rice. Continue baking until bottoms are browned, about 3 to 4 minutes. Fill as desired.

Mushroom Tart

8 to 10 servings

Chive Pastry
1½ cups unbleached all purpose flour (7½ ounces)
½ teaspoon salt
½ cup (1 stick) unsalted butter, well chilled
5 tablespoons cold water
1 egg yolk
1 tablespoon snipped fresh chives

Filling
¼ cup (½ stick) unsalted butter
2 tablespoons oil
8 ounces mushrooms, caps sliced, stems chopped

12 medium green onions (6 ounces total), thinly sliced
1 tablespoon flour

5 ounces Swiss cheese, shredded (1¼ cups)
1 cup half and half
4 eggs
1 whole canned pimiento (1½ ounces), pureed
¾ to 1 teaspoon salt
Freshly ground pepper

For pastry: Combine flour and salt in mixing bowl. Cut in butter until mixture resembles coarse meal. Add water, yolk and chives and mix with fork until dough holds together. Transfer to plastic bag. Shape into ball, then flatten into disc. Chill at least 2 hours.

Butter 11-inch quiche pan with removable bottom. Roll dough out on lightly floured surface to thickness of ⅛ inch. Place in pan, pressing around bottom and sides. Trim 1 inch beyond rim (reserve scraps); fold back against inside to form double thickness extending crust ¼ inch above edge of pan. Pinch to form decorative edge. Prick bottom and sides with fork and chill pastry until firm, about 30 minutes.

About 15 minutes before baking, preheat oven to 400°F. Line pastry with parchment paper and fill with rice or dried beans. Bake 12 minutes. Remove paper and beans. Prick crust again. Bake until lightly browned, about 6 minutes. Carefully remove from pan and cool on wire rack. Repair any cracks by patching with leftover scraps of dough.

For filling: Position rack in center of oven and preheat to 375°F. Melt butter with oil in large skillet over medium-high heat. Add mushrooms and cook until liquid is evaporated, about 8 minutes. Add onion and cook 3 minutes. Blend in flour and cook an additional 3 minutes. Remove from heat.

Sprinkle crust with cheese. Whisk half and half, eggs, pimiento and seasoning in large bowl. Add mushroom mixture. Spoon into crust, filling to within ⅛ inch of top. Bake until deeply golden, about 30 to 40 minutes. Let stand for 10 minutes before slicing, or serve at room temperature.

Spiced Spinach Pie

Perfect for a picnic brunch, this quiche can be baked a day ahead and refrigerated.

6 servings

Pastry
¾ cup unbleached all purpose flour
⅓ cup cake flour
⅛ teaspoon salt
6 tablespoons (¾ stick) unsalted butter, chilled and cut into small pieces
3 to 4 tablespoons ice water

Spinach Filling
1 bunch (about 13 ounces) fresh spinach, stems discarded

3 tablespoons unsalted butter
1 medium onion, minced
2 garlic cloves, minced
⅓ cup pine nuts or sunflower seeds, toasted

¼ cup golden raisins
Generous pinch of cinnamon
Salt and freshly ground pepper
Freshly grated nutmeg

4 ounces cream cheese, room temperature
1 cup sour cream
4 eggs
⅛ teaspoon salt
Generous pinch of freshly ground pepper
Generous pinch of ground red pepper

6 ounces freshly grated Parmesan cheese

For pastry: Combine flours and salt in processor and mix well. Add butter and blend using on/off turns until mixture resembles coarse meal. Add water and mix using on/off turns just until dough begins to mass together. Gather dough into ball, wrap in plastic and refrigerate 1 to 24 hours. (To mix by hand, combine flours and salt in deep bowl. Cut in butter using pastry blender until mixture resembles coarse meal. Add water and toss mixture with fork until moistened. Gather dough into ball, wrap and refrigerate 1 to 24 hours.)

Grease 10-inch pie plate or 6-cup quiche dish and set aside. Roll dough out on lightly floured surface into large circle ⅛ inch thick. Fit into prepared pie plate and flute edges. Chill 1 to 8 hours.

Preheat oven to 400°F. Line pastry with foil and weight with dried beans or rice. Bake 10 minutes. Discard foil and beans and continue baking until crust is golden brown, about 4 minutes. Cool.

For spinach filling: Wash spinach thoroughly and transfer to large saucepan. Cook over medium-high heat, using only water clinging to leaves, until spinach is wilted. Plunge immediately into ice water to stop cooking process. Drain and pat dry. Chop finely and set aside.

Position rack in lower third of oven and preheat to 350°F. Melt butter in large saucepan over medium-high heat. Add onion and sauté until golden brown. Stir in garlic, nuts and raisins and cook 1 minute. Add spinach, cinnamon, salt, pepper and nutmeg and cook, stirring constantly, until moisture has evaporated, about 1 minute. Set aside.

Combine cream cheese, sour cream, eggs, salt, pepper and red pepper in processor or blender and puree.

Spread spinach mixture over bottom of crust. Sprinkle with Parmesan cheese. Pour cream cheese mixture over top. Bake until knife inserted between edge and center of filling comes out clean, about 40 minutes. Cool to room temperature, cover and refrigerate.

For a variation, combine spinach mixture and Parmesan cheese and spoon into fresh mushroom caps. Bake at 400°F until filling is hot and bubbly. Serve hot or cold.

Zewelwai (Onion Pie)

This is a variation of quiche made in both Alsace and Lorraine; bacon is likely to be found in the Lorraine version, while Alsatians tend to prefer the taste of onions alone. In the springtime it is a nice idea to use green onions, including some of the stem.

6 to 8 servings

Crust
2 cups all purpose flour
½ cup (1 stick) butter, room temperature
½ teaspoon salt
4 tablespoons (about) cold water

Filling
3 tablespoons goose fat, chicken fat or butter

3 to 4 medium onions, thinly sliced
3½ ounces bacon (optional), diced and parboiled 1 minute
3 eggs
½ cup whipping cream
½ teaspoon caraway seed (optional)
Salt and freshly ground pepper
Freshly grated nutmeg

For crust: Combine flour, butter and salt with hands until mixture resembles small peas. Add water, working the dough as little as possible, and form into ball, adding more water if necessary to make dough soft but not sticky. Knead lightly until smooth and pliable by pushing dough away with heel of hand and then gathering it up with dough scraper. Flatten into disc, wrap tightly and chill 1½ to 2 hours.

Roll out dough on lightly floured surface. Line 10-inch quiche dish or pie pan, crimping edges to fit. Prick bottom and sides with fork. Chill thoroughly.

Preheat oven to 375°F. Line dough with waxed or parchment paper and fill with dried beans or rice. Bake until pastry is firm and just beginning to brown, about 15 to 20 minutes. Remove paper, beans or rice and let pastry cool.

Meanwhile, make filling: Melt fat in large skillet over very low heat. Add onions and cook, stirring occasionally, until completely softened *but not brown,* about 20 to 30 minutes. Spread onions over crust and sprinkle with bacon. Beat eggs, cream, caraway, salt, pepper and nutmeg together and pour into crust. Bake until filling is set and golden brown, about 40 to 45 minutes; *do not overcook or filling will curdle.* Serve warm or at room temperature.

Quiche Alsacienne aux Fruits (Alsatian Fruit Quiche)

6 to 8 servings

Pastry
1½ cups all purpose flour
⅓ cup unsalted butter
1 egg yolk
4½ to 5½ tablespoons cold water
¾ teaspoon salt

Fruit
3 tablespoons butter
2 pounds tart apples or pears, peeled, cored and sliced*
1 tablespoon sugar

Syrup
2 cups water
½ cup sugar or to taste

1 vanilla bean, split and scraped
Juice and grated peel of 1 lemon

Custard
2 eggs
1 egg yolk
½ cup sugar
6 tablespoons whipping cream
¼ cup milk
½ teaspoon vanilla or 1 teaspoon kirsch

1 egg white

Glaze
⅓ cup strained apricot preserves

For pastry: Sift flour onto marble slab or other working surface and make a large well in center. Pound butter to soften slightly. Place butter, yolk, 4½ tablespoons water and salt into well and work together with fingertips until partially mixed. Gradually work in the flour until dough is size of large crumbs. If crumbs are dry, sprinkle with an additional tablespoon of cold water; dough should be soft but not sticky. Press together firmly.

Lightly flour working surface. Work dough until smooth and pliable by pushing it away with heel of hand and then gathering up with dough scraper. Press into 8-inch circle, cover with plastic wrap and chill 30 minutes to 1 hour.

For fruit: If using apples, melt butter in large saucepan over medium heat. Add apples and sauté until softened, about 5 minutes. Sprinkle with sugar and continue cooking until sugar is lightly caramelized. Remove from heat.

If using pears, combine all ingredients for syrup and cook over medium heat, stirring until sugar is dissolved. Add fruit and poach until barely tender. Cool in syrup; drain before using.

For custard: Beat eggs, yolk and sugar until thoroughly mixed. Add cream, milk, vanilla or kirsch and blend well.

To assemble: Place oven rack in lowest position and preheat to 400°F. Roll out pastry on lightly floured surface. Fit into 10-inch flan ring or pie pan and flute edges. Prick bottom and sides of shell with fork. Cover bottom with waxed paper or foil and fill with dried beans or rice. Bake 20 minutes.

Remove from oven and discard paper and beans or rice. Reduce oven temperature to 375°F. Beat egg white lightly and brush on pastry. Arrange fruit in shell. Spoon custard over top. Bake until custard is set, about 40 minutes, covering edges of pastry with foil if it begins to brown too quickly. Cool to room temperature on wire rack.

When filling is cool, melt preserves in small saucepan. Brush quiche with glaze and let set before serving.

*Pitted bing cherries, Italian, greengage or purple plums, or apricots can be substituted. Poach in syrup as for pears. If using purple plums or apricots, the fruit should be arranged cut side up in the pie shell. The juices produced during cooking will evaporate rather than drain into the custard and make the pastry soggy.

Broccoli-Cauliflower Pie

6 main-course servings or 8 first-course or side-dish servings

1 pound broccoli, separated into florets
1 pound cauliflower, separated into florets

2 tablespoons olive oil
1 large onion, chopped
1 large garlic clove, minced
   Salt and freshly ground pepper

Wheat Germ Pastry (see following recipe)

6 ounces Swiss cheese, grated
6 ounces freshly grated imported Asiago cheese
1 egg, beaten

Divide broccoli and cauliflower florets into small pieces. Peel stems of broccoli and thinly slice into rounds.

Heat oil in large skillet over medium heat. Add onion and sauté until soft. Add garlic, broccoli and cauliflower. Increase heat to medium-high and sauté about 4 minutes. Season to taste with salt and pepper. Remove from heat and let cool while making pastry.

Position rack in lower third of oven and preheat to 400°F. Grease 9 × 1¾-inch pan with removable bottom.

Roll out ⅔ of pastry on floured surface to fit pan, leaving ½-inch overhang. Line pan and chill 30 minutes.

Combine vegetables and cheeses and toss lightly. Spoon into crust. Roll out remaining pastry to cover top. Trim and seal pastry, reserving scraps for decoration, if desired. Cut hole in center of top and brush pastry with egg. Bake until top is browned, about 1 hour. Unmold and serve immediately.

Any vegetable may be used with this dish. Try combining leftovers with cheese and a bit of béchamel sauce and bake. Here are a few suggestions:

Combine parsnips, carrots, garlic, fresh ginger and sesame seed and stir-fry before tossing with Gruyère or Swiss cheese.

Sauté cabbage, onion and sweet red pepper and mix with a little basil-seasoned béchamel.

Blend salsify, green onions, fontinella cheese, béchamel and fresh tarragon.

Chop leftover green beans and mix with cashews, Parmesan cheese and a dash of sour cream.

Wheat Germ Pastry

Makes pastry for 1 pie

1¾ cups unbleached all purpose flour
¼ cup wheat germ
¼ teaspoon salt
6 tablespoons well-chilled unsalted butter

5 tablespoons well-chilled solid shortening
4 to 5 tablespoons cold water

Follow four basic steps in Pastry Primer (see box, page 22).

Cauliflower, Carrot and Parmesan Quiche

Makes one 9-inch quiche

1 partially baked 9 × 1½-inch pastry crust
1½ cups (6 ounces) shredded Parmesan cheese
1½ cups coarsely chopped fresh cauliflower, cooked just until tender, drained well

½ cup ¼-inch julienne of fresh carrot, cooked just until tender, drained well
3 eggs
1½ cups whipping cream
Salt and hot pepper sauce

Preheat oven to 300°F. Sprinkle crust with half of cheese. Add cauliflower and carrot, distributing evenly, reserving 10 carrot slices for decoration if desired. Sprinkle vegetables with remaining cheese. Lightly beat eggs in medium bowl. Stir in cream. Add salt and pepper sauce to taste. Pour over vegetables. Arrange reserved carrot in circle over top. Bake until top is lightly browned and custard is set, about 1 hour (cover edge of pastry with foil if necessary to prevent excessive browning). Let stand at room temperature about 15 minutes; slice into wedges and serve.

For best results, prepare partially baked crust in 9 × 1½-inch cake pan with removable bottom.

Asparagus Tart with Hollandaise Sauce

6 to 8 servings

2 pounds asparagus spears (ends discarded), peeled*

4 tablespoons light vegetable oil (preferably cold-pressed safflower)

½ pound firm mushrooms, thinly sliced

1 teaspoon fresh lemon juice

3 tablespoons whole wheat pastry flour

1¾ cups milk or half and half

¼ cup finely chopped prosciutto (optional)

4 tablespoons freshly grated Parmesan cheese
Herb or vegetable salt
Freshly ground white pepper

Hollandaise Sauce
2 egg yolks
2 tablespoons fresh lemon juice
2 tablespoons half and half, sour cream or plain yogurt
¼ teaspoon herb or vegetable salt
½ cup light vegetable oil

2 tablespoons dry whole wheat breadcrumbs

1 10- or 11-inch baked Whole Wheat Short Pastry shell (see recipe, p. 27)

Steam asparagus until just crisp-tender, about 4 minutes. Drain well and set aside. Heat 1 tablespoon oil in medium skillet over high heat. Add mushrooms and lemon juice and stir-fry 1 minute. With slotted spoon remove mushrooms from skillet and set aside.

Combine 3 tablespoons oil with flour in small saucepan and stir over low heat until mixture is just bubbling, about 2 to 3 minutes. Remove from heat and blend in milk. Place over medium heat and bring to boil, stirring constantly until thickened. Blend in prosciutto and 2 tablespoons cheese. Add mushrooms. Season with herb salt and pepper to taste. Reduce heat to low and stir until cheese is completely melted.

For hollandaise sauce: Combine egg yolks, lemon juice, half and half and herb salt in small bowl and beat with small whisk. Set bowl in medium skillet half-filled with hot water. Beat mixture over low heat until thick, about 5 minutes. Whisking constantly, gradually add ½ cup oil in slow steady stream. Remove from water bath and let stand at room temperature.

To assemble: Sprinkle breadcrumbs and remaining 2 tablespoons cheese over bottom of pastry shell. Spoon mushroom sauce over crumbs, spreading evenly. Arrange asparagus spears in spoke pattern over top. Cover with hollandaise sauce. Just before serving, lightly brown tart under broiler, about 1 to 2 minutes, watching closely to prevent hollandaise sauce from separating. Serve tart immediately.

*One 10-ounce box frozen asparagus can be substituted for fresh. Cook in boiling water until crisp-tender, about 4 minutes.

Zucchini Quiche

10 servings

10 eggs
2 quarts (8 cups) finely chopped
zucchini (about 2½ pounds)
2 cups buttermilk baking mix
1 onion, finely chopped

1 cup oil
1 cup grated Parmesan cheese
1 teaspoon garlic powder
1 teaspoon garlic salt

Position rack in lower third of oven and preheat to 350°F. Grease 11 × 17-inch baking pan. Beat eggs in large bowl. Add remaining ingredients and mix well. Pour into pan. Bake until tester inserted in center comes out clean, about 35 minutes. Cool slightly before cutting into squares.

Gibanica (Serbian Cheese Pie)

12 first-course servings

½ pound Kajmak (see following
recipe) or mild Camembert or
Brie, crust removed
½ pound cream cheese (room
temperature), cut into chunks
5 eggs, separated

Pinch of salt
Pinch of cream of tartar

1 quart (4 cups) milk
Salt

1 pound phyllo leaves (preferably
fresh, not frozen)
⅓ cup vegetable oil
1 teaspoon olive oil

Preheat oven to 400°F. Lightly oil or grease 9 × 13-inch baking dish. Combine kajmak and cream cheese in large bowl and blend well. Beat in egg yolks.

Beat egg whites until foamy. Add salt and cream of tartar and continue beating until stiff. Carefully fold into cheese, blending gently but completely. Mix in milk and salt until thick and creamy.

Dip 1 sheet of phyllo into cheese mixture and place in bottom of baking dish. Repeat until 3 sheets of pastry remain. Pour half of remaining cheese mixture into dish. Combine oils and use to brush remaining phyllo generously. Add to dish. Pour in remaining cheese.

Bake about 40 minutes, piercing with fork several times during baking until top is golden and pastry has shrunk slightly from sides of dish. Serve hot.

Kajmak

For best results unhomogenized whole milk really should be used for this popular cheese, but since it is not readily available, this version combines regular whole milk and half and half.

1 quart (4 cups) homogenized
whole milk

2 cups half and half
Salt

Combine milk and half and half in saucepan and bring to boil. Pour into wide shallow bowl. As the milk cools, a layer of cream resembling the "skin" on scalded milk will rise to surface. Remove this layer and place in crock or similar container. Sprinkle with salt. Repeat boiling, skimming and salting twice a day, until you have as much kajmak as desired. (After 4 days you will have about ½ cup.)

At this stage the cheese is called "young" kajmak and is white and very delicate in flavor. As kajmak ages it ferments and more salt is added to help preserve it. The color also becomes yellow and the flavor more definite.

The day before serving kajmak, place in cheesecloth-lined strainer and drain overnight. Mound in ball to serve.

2 ❦ Seafood, Poultry and Meat Entrées

A brunch or breakfast menu can be small and simple, but it can also be as big and complex as any dinner. More and more, the morning meal is being used as a focus for entertaining, either in the shape of a buffet or as a multicourse, all-stops-out production. In these cases, one or more entrées is usually required, and the host or hostess will look for something substantial that is suitable to the time of day. A number of egg dishes work well, obviously, but there are other possibilities; and the seafood, poultry and meat recipes that follow fit the bill perfectly.

Salmon, long a staple of the European breakfast table, is a favorite breakfast fish. It can be simply marinated—as in the recipe for traditional Swedish Gravlax (page 37)—or poached and served cold with a delicate Avocado Cream (page 36). For a more substantial dish, try a combination of seafoods: the strudel on page 36 combines mixed fish and shellfish with Swiss cheese and sour cream in a delicious treat.

Poultry and meat dishes appeal to heartier appetites. Prepared with an herb butter and napped with Cognac-laced Sauce Chivry, Chicken Breasts Wrapped in Endive (page 39) make a truly elegant entrée with a Belgian flavor. Or, as a substitute for *foie gras*, try seared chicken livers with a piquant chive vinaigrette (page 38)—very light but very rich. Mild or hot, there is nothing quite like homemade sausages. On pages 41–45 you'll find recipes for simple links and patties, for Italian, Mexican and German sausages, and even one version flavored with Champagne. If you don't want to make your own sausage, there is Saucisson en Croute (page 46)—green onions and mushrooms mixed with pork sausage and wrapped in buttery puff pastry.

Corned beef hash, when served up in baked potato shells with a tomato-butter sauce, gives a sophistication far above its homely origins. For ham lovers there is a do-ahead glazed loaf that is excellent with any kind of eggs. And last, but certainly not least, bacon: Try it in Schnitzen (page 48), an Alsatian specialty that includes dried fruits and potatoes for a dish that will take any menu out of the ordinary.

Seafood

Cold Poached Salmon with Avocado Cream

6 servings

Avocado Cream
2 ripe avocados, pitted, peeled and coarsely chopped
2 medium-size green onions, chopped
½ cup plus 2 tablespoons mayonnaise (preferably homemade)
¼ cup plain yogurt
3 tablespoons fresh lemon juice
½ teaspoon minced garlic
2 tablespoons chopped fresh parsley
12 fresh coriander leaves (cilantro) or ¼ teaspoon dried, crumbled
Salt and freshly ground pepper

Salmon
4 cups fish stock or clam broth
2 cups fruity white wine (preferably Chenin Blanc or French Colombard)
6 peppercorns
1 carrot, coarsely chopped
1 large onion, coarsely chopped
1 bay leaf
3 coriander seeds
Generous pinch of dried thyme
6 6- to 8-ounce salmon fillets, skinned and boned
¼ cup vegetable oil
2 tablespoons fresh lemon juice

1 large head romaine lettuce, separated into leaves, rinsed and patted dry

Salt and freshly ground pepper
3 tablespoons chopped chives (garnish)
10 chive flowers (optional garnish)

For avocado cream: Combine all ingredients in processor or blender and puree. Transfer to jar with tight-fitting lid and refrigerate up to 2 days.

For salmon: Combine fish stock, wine, peppercorns, carrot, onion, bay leaf, coriander and thyme in large saucepan and bring to boil over medium-high heat, skimming foam as it accumulates. Cover partially, reduce heat and simmer about 30 minutes. Strain stock through colander into large skillet. Place over medium heat and bring to gentle simmer. Reduce heat to low, add salmon and poach until almost cooked through, about 6 minutes. Remove from heat and let fish cool in stock. Drain fillets well. Arrange in single layer in shallow baking pan. Sprinkle with oil and lemon juice. Cover and refrigerate overnight.

Cut romaine crosswise into very thin strips. Wrap in paper towel and chill.

To assemble: Drain salmon and pat dry with paper towels. Arrange shredded romaine over bottom of large shallow container and top with salmon. Sprinkle lightly with salt and pepper. Cover and refrigerate. Just before serving, top with avocado cream and garnish with chives and chive flowers.

Seafood Strudel

Makes 6 to 8 servings

2 tablespoons (¼ stick) unsalted butter
2 tablespoons all purpose flour
½ teaspoon Dijon mustard

Salt
Cayenne pepper
¾ cup milk, room temperature
2 tablespoons whipping cream

1 cup breadcrumbs
¼ cup freshly grated Parmesan cheese
¼ teaspoon dry mustard
1 pound cleaned, shelled cooked crab, shrimp, lobster or halibut, or combination, in bite-size chunks
½ pound phyllo pastry sheets
½ cup grated Swiss cheese
2 hard-cooked eggs, chopped
¾ cup sour cream
¼ cup chopped parsley

¼ cup diced shallots
2 tablespoons chopped chives
1 large garlic clove, minced

¾ cup (1½ sticks) unsalted butter, melted
2 tablespoons chopped parsley

2 tablespoons freshly grated Parmesan cheese
Minced parsley
Crab or lobster claws (optional garnish)

Melt 2 tablespoons butter in small saucepan over low heat. Stir in flour to make smooth paste and heat gently, stirring constantly, until mixture just begins to bubble. Remove from heat and add mustard, pinch of salt and cayenne pepper. Slowly stir in milk. Place over medium heat and cook, stirring constantly, until mixture bubbles and thickens. Add cream, taste for seasonings and adjust if necessary. Cover and chill until very thick and firm, about 2 hours.

Preheat oven to 375°F; butter baking sheet. Combine breadcrumbs, Parmesan and dry mustard in small bowl. Layer seafood evenly on phyllo and sprinkle with Swiss cheese and chopped egg. Dot with sour cream. Sprinkle with parsley, shallots, chives and garlic and dot with chilled sauce.

Roll as directed (see box, page 82–83), place on prepared baking sheet and brush with some of melted butter. Bake 12 minutes. Remove from oven and brush with more melted butter. Slice diagonally with serrated knife into 1½-inch pieces. Push slices together to reshape loaf. Add parsley to remaining butter and brush again. Repeat brushing 3 more times during baking, reserving a little butter to brush on just before serving. Bake 35 to 40 minutes longer, until crisp and golden brown. Meanwhile, warm large serving platter.

Remove strudel from oven and brush with remaining parsley butter. Cool 10 minutes and transfer to warmed serving platter using long spatula. Dust with Parmesan and minced parsley. Garnish with crab or lobster claws, if desired.

Gravlax

Salmon is the star attraction in this Swedish favorite. Serve it within 5 days of the initial preparation.

8 servings

3 pounds fresh center-cut salmon *(do not substitute other fish)*
1 cup fresh dill sprigs, chopped or ⅓ cup dried dillweed
¼ cup sugar
2 tablespoons salt
2 tablespoons freshly ground white pepper

2 tablespoons oil

Lemon slices, cherry tomatoes and fresh dill or watercress sprigs (garnish)
Sweet Mustard Sauce or Mustard Mayonnaise (see following recipes)

Cut salmon in half lengthwise into 2 equal pieces. (For easier slicing, remove any remaining bones from salmon with tweezer.) Combine dill, sugar, salt and pepper and blend well. Brush oil on fillets and sprinkle dill mixture evenly over *cut* surfaces *(not on skin)*. Place half of fish, skin side down, on large piece of foil. Place other fish half, skin side up, on top of bottom piece. Wrap entirely in foil and set in glass, enamel or stainless steel dish. Weight heavily with bricks. Chill at least 48 hours. Three times during this period unwrap, turn salmon over, baste fillets with accumulated juices and rewrap tightly.

Within 5 days, scrape away dill and pat salmon dry. Slice *paper thin* on diagonal with sharp knife, separating salmon from skin. Arrange slices on platter and garnish with lemon, cherry tomatoes and dill or watercress. Serve with Sweet Mustard Sauce or Mustard Mayonnaise.

Sweet Mustard Sauce

Makes ⅔ cup

2 tablespoons plus 1 teaspoon white vinegar	1½ teaspoons dry mustard
2 tablespoons sugar	⅓ cup safflower oil
4 teaspoons Dijon mustard	3 tablespoons chopped fresh dill

Combine first 4 ingredients in food processor or blender and mix well. With machine running, slowly add oil until sauce is thickened (remaining oil can be added more quickly). Transfer to serving bowl and garnish with dill.

Sauce can also be mixed with whisk, incorporating oil 1 tablespoon at a time.

Mustard Mayonnaise

Makes 1¾ cups

1 egg	1 teaspoon fresh lemon juice
1 egg yolk	½ teaspoon dry mustard
1 tablespoon Dijon mustard	1½ cups oil
1 teaspoon salt	½ cup whipping cream
1 teaspoon red wine vinegar	

Combine first 7 ingredients with 3 tablespoons oil in food processor or blender and mix until slightly thickened. With machine running, slowly add remaining oil in steady stream until mayonnaise thickens. Add cream; mix until combined.

 Poultry

Seared Chicken Livers with Chives

These chicken livers are prepared in the manner of fresh foie gras.

6 servings

1 pound fresh chicken livers, membranes trimmed	**Hot Vinaigrette**
1 cup milk	2 tablespoons walnut oil
1 teaspoon salt	2 tablespoons red wine vinegar
Freshly ground pepper	2 tablespoons Port
¾ cup unbleached all purpose flour	4 tablespoons freshly snipped chives
2 to 3 tablespoons unsalted butter	
2 to 3 tablespoons oil	

Soak chicken livers in milk 30 minutes. Drain and pat dry with paper towels. Sprinkle livers on both sides with salt and pepper. Dip into flour, covering completely; shake off excess.

Heat 2 tablespoons butter and 2 tablespoons oil in sauté pan or skillet over medium-high heat until sizzling. Add liver in batches (do not crowd) and cook until encrusted on underside, then turn and repeat on other side. (Total cooking time is about 4 minutes.) Livers should be crisp on outside, soft and barely pink on inside. Set aside and keep warm. Repeat procedure until all livers are cooked, adding remaining butter and oil if necessary.

Meanwhile, combine walnut oil, vinegar and Port and bring just to boil. Remove from heat and stir in 3 tablespoons chives. Place livers in serving dish. Spoon hot vinaigrette over top and garnish with remaining chives.

Chicken Breasts Wrapped in Endive with Herb Butter and Sauce Chivry

4 servings

Sauce Chivry
1 cup dry white wine or vermouth
1 small shallot, minced
1 small garlic clove, minced
1 tablespoon minced fresh chervil or 1 teaspoon dried, crumbled
1 tablespoon minced fresh thyme or 1 teaspoon dried, crumbled
1 tablespoon minced fresh tarragon or 1 teaspoon dried, crumbled
1 tablespoon minced fresh parsley

2 tablespoons (¼ stick) butter
2 tablespoons flour
2 cups chicken stock

½ cup whipping cream
2 egg yolks
2 tablespoons Cognac
   Juice of ½ lemon
1 tablespoon minced fresh chives or minced green onion
⅛ teaspoon freshly grated nutmeg
   Salt and freshly ground pepper

Herb Butter
¼ cup (½ stick) butter
2 tablespoons minced fresh chives or minced green onion
1 small garlic clove, minced or pressed
1 tablespoon minced fresh chervil or 1 teaspoon dried, crumbled
1 tablespoon minced fresh thyme or 1 teaspoon dried, crumbled
1 tablespoon minced fresh tarragon or 1 teaspoon dried, crumbled
1 tablespoon minced fresh parsley
   Juice of ½ lemon

1 pound Belgian endive

2 large whole chicken breasts, halved
   Salt and freshly ground pepper

2 tablespoons (¼ stick) butter, cut into small pieces

For sauce: Combine first 7 ingredients in small saucepan and boil over high heat until reduced to ⅓ cup. Set aside.

Melt butter in heavy saucepan over low heat. Whisk in flour and let foam 3 minutes without coloring, stirring constantly. Whisk in chicken stock and stir over medium-high heat until sauce comes to boil. Reduce heat and simmer, stirring occasionally, until reduced by half, about 1 hour. Strain.

Mix whipping cream and egg yolks in small bowl. Slowly whisk in sauce. Return to pan. Press reduced herb mixture through a strainer into sauce. Add Cognac and bring to boil over medium-high heat, stirring constantly. Blend in lemon juice, chives, nutmeg, salt and pepper. Taste and adjust seasoning. Keep warm in bain-marie.

Preheat oven to 400°F. Butter 9 × 12-inch baking dish; set aside.

For herb butter: Melt butter over low heat with chives, garlic, chervil, thyme, tarragon and parsley. Stir in lemon juice. Remove from heat and cool slightly.

Separate endive into individual leaves. Cook in large pot of boiling salted water until wilted, about 3 minutes. Drain and refresh under cold water. Spin dry in salad spinner or pat dry.

Skin and bone chicken breasts; remove tendons. Lightly pound breasts between two sheets of waxed paper until chicken is uniform thickness. Brush one side of chicken with cooled herb butter and sprinkle with salt and pepper. Cover with about half of blanched endive leaves, pressing until they adhere to chicken. Arrange endive side down in baking dish. Brush tops with melted herb butter, sprinkle with salt and pepper and cover with more endive leaves. Bake for 20 minutes.

Whisk remaining butter into sauce bit by bit, blending well after each addition and making sure butter is completely incorporated before adding more. Pour over chicken and serve immediately.

 *Meats*

Corned Beef Hash in Baked Potato Shells with Fresh Tomato Butter Sauce

6 servings

3 large Idaho potatoes, scrubbed, dried and buttered

1 tablespoon butter
1 tablespoon oil
1 small Spanish onion, finely minced (5 ounces)
3 large scallions, thinly sliced (2½ ounces)
½ pound cooked corned beef, cut into ¼-inch cubes
3 tablespoons chicken broth
1½ teaspoons Worcestershire sauce
¼ teaspoon freshly grated nutmeg
   Dash of hot pepper sauce
   Salt and freshly ground pepper

2 ounces cheddar cheese, shredded
2 tablespoons freshly snipped chives
4 tablespoons parsley leaves, minced

1½ pounds broccoli (3 cups florets; reserve stems for another use)
2 tablespoons (¼ stick) butter
½ teaspoon salt
¼ teaspoon freshly grated nutmeg
   Freshly ground pepper
6 eggs

   Fresh Tomato Butter Sauce (see following recipe)

Preheat oven to 425°F. Bake potatoes until just soft, about 1 hour; *do not overbake*. Cool 20 minutes. Halve potatoes horizontally and carefully scoop out pulp, keeping it in chunks as large as possible and leaving ⅛-inch shell. *This can be done 1 day ahead; wrap shells and pulp tightly in plastic and refrigerate.*

Preheat oven to 350°F. Cut potato pulp into ¼-inch dice. Heat butter and oil in large skillet over medium-high heat until sizzling. Add onion and scallion and sauté 3 minutes. Add diced potato and corned beef and toss gently for an additional 3 minutes. Add broth, Worcestershire, nutmeg, hot pepper sauce, salt and pepper and cook 2 minutes, stirring frequently. Remove from heat and add cheese, chives and 3 tablespoons parsley. Taste and adjust seasoning.

Carefully mound mixture in scooped-out potato halves. Cover each with foil "cap" and set in ovenproof dish. (Do not cover dish with foil; it creates too much moisture.) *Hash can be prepared in advance to this point. If made in advance and refrigerated, bring to room temperature before baking.* Bake 30 minutes.

Meanwhile, cook florets in 3 quarts boiling salted water for 3 minutes. Drain and immediately plunge into ice water. When completely cold to the touch, drain.

At serving time, heat butter in large skillet over high heat until bubbly. Add broccoli, salt, nutmeg and pepper and toss 2 minutes. Taste and adjust seasoning. Poach eggs.

Arrange potatoes on heated platter. Top each with poached egg and sprinkle with remaining parsley. Garnish platter with broccoli. Serve immediately with hot Fresh Tomato Butter Sauce.

Poached eggs can be prepared up to 2 days in advance. Immerse uncooked eggs still in their shells in pot of boiling water for 10 seconds. Remove with slotted spoon. Fill large skillet with 2 inches of water. Add 2 tablespoons vinegar. Bring to simmer over medium heat. Carefully break eggs into skillet and poach 3 minutes. If egg is not holding its shape, mold with 2 large spoons. Remove each egg with slotted spoon to bowl of cold water to stop cooking process and eliminate any vinegar taste. After cooling, if edges of eggs are ragged, trim with kitchen shears. Cover bowl and chill. To reheat, bring eggs to room temperature. Place eggs one at a time in strainer and dip into pan of boiling water for about 1 minute. Pat bottom of strainer with towel to absorb all of the excess moisture.

Fresh Tomato Butter Sauce

Sauce can be made ahead to point of adding butter. Bring just to boiling before adding butter and completing sauce.

Makes 1½ cups

4 **large tomatoes (about 1½ pounds), peeled, seeded and coarsely chopped**
¼ **cup minced shallots (about 4 large)**
3 **tablespoons tomato paste**
1 **small garlic clove, minced**
2 **teaspoons sugar**
1½ **teaspoons salt**
1 **teaspoon dry mustard**

1 **teaspoon dried basil**
1 **teaspoon dried oregano**
Freshly ground pepper
½ **cup plus 2 tablespoons (1¼ sticks) chilled unsalted butter, cut into tablespoon-size pieces**
3 **tablespoons freshly snipped chives**
2 **tablespoons minced fresh parsley leaves**

Combine first 10 ingredients in medium saucepan. Place over high heat and cook, stirring frequently, until excess liquid has evaporated and mixture resembles soft marmalade, about 8 to 10 minutes. Add 2 tablespoons butter and whisk thoroughly. When butter is almost melted and incorporated, add 2 more tablespoons, repeating until all butter is used. Do not allow sauce to boil. Adjust seasoning. Pour into sauceboat and stir in chives. Sprinkle with parsley and serve.

Homemade Sausage Patties

2 servings

1 **pound fresh pork***
1 **teaspoon powdered sage**
¾ **teaspoon salt**
¾ **teaspoon freshly ground pepper**
Pinch of ground allspice

Pinch of ground red pepper
Pinch of finely minced bay leaf

1 **ounce blanched pistachio nuts, chopped**

Cut pork into 1-inch cubes. Grind finely with meat grinder or in food processor. Transfer to medium bowl. Add sage, salt, pepper, allspice, red pepper and bay leaf and mix thoroughly.

Heat skillet over medium-high heat. Drop 1 tablespoon of mixture into skillet and brown, turning once. Taste and adjust seasoning for uncooked mixture. Blend in pistachios. Form into patties. Sauté in skillet until well browned on both sides and cooked to desired doneness. Serve immediately.

* For best results, pork should be at least 25 percent fat. Add more fat if too lean.

Breakfast Sausages

*Shape sausages into patties
or use casings. Serve with
Mashed Potatoes with Sor-
rel and Apples and Sautéed
Apples.*

*4 to 6 servings (about 12
sausages)*

1½ **pounds trimmed pork shoulder or
loin, cut into ½ × 1¾-inch strips**
½ **pound trimmed pork fat, cut into
½ × 1¾-inch strips**
½ **small onion, sliced**
2 **medium garlic cloves**
1½ **tablespoons minced fresh sage or
1⅛ teaspoons dried, crumbled**
1½ **teaspoons minced fresh savory or
½ teaspoon dried, crumbled**
2 **teaspoons salt**

¼ **teaspoon freshly ground pepper**
¼ **cup (4 tablespoons) whipping
cream, milk or dry white wine**

2½ **quarts water**
1 **tablespoon butter**
1 **tablespoon oil**

**Mashed Potatoes with Sorrel and
Apples (see following recipe)
Sautéed Apples (see following
recipe)**

If using casings, rinse them and soak in tepid water for 1 hour. Freeze pork and
fat for 30 minutes, then grind through fine blade of grinder with onion and garlic.
Mix in sage, savory, salt and pepper. Stir in cream 1 tablespoon at a time. Cover
and chill 1 hour.

Form sausage mixture into patties or stuff into casings and tie or twist into
12 links. Hang links in a cool spot until dry or refrigerate patties on a rack, turning
occasionally, 12 to 24 hours.

To cook links: Bring water to simmer in Dutch oven or large saucepan. Add
sausages, cover and poach gently 15 minutes. Drain sausages well, discarding
poaching liquid. Pat sausages dry. Heat butter and oil in same saucepan. Add
sausages and sauté over medium heat until brown on all sides.

To cook patties: Melt butter with oil in heavy large skillet over medium-
high heat. Add sausages in batches and fry on both sides until browned and cooked
through. Drain on paper towels.

To serve: Divide Mashed Potatoes with Sorrel and Apples among 4 heated
plates. Surround with cooked sausages and hot Sautéed Apples.

Mashed Potatoes with Sorrel and Apples

2 **tablespoons (¼ stick) butter**
2 **pounds apples, peeled, cored and
sliced**
⅓ **cup whipping cream**
⅓ **cup Calvados, applejack or apple
cider
Sugar**

2 **pounds boiling potatoes, peeled
and quartered**

10 **large sorrel or spinach leaves,
stemmed and cut into chiffonade**
2 **teaspoons apple cider vinegar or
to taste
Salt and freshly ground pepper
Freshly grated nutmeg**

Melt butter in heavy large skillet over medium-high heat. Add apples, cover and
cook, stirring occasionally, until almost tender, about 20 minutes. Add cream,
Calvados and sugar to taste and cook 15 minutes more, mashing mixture occasionally to puree.

Cook potatoes in large pot of boiling salted water until tender. Drain. Push
through sieve with mallet using straight up and down motion to prevent their
becoming glutinous. Sieve apple puree into potatoes and blend well.

Rinse sorrel; shake off excess water. Place in skillet over medium-high heat
and stir until wilted. Blend into potato-apple puree. Season with vinegar, salt,
pepper and nutmeg. Just before serving, stir over high heat to warm through.

Sautéed Apples

2 tablespoons (¼ stick) butter
2 large apples, peeled, cored and sliced

2 teaspoons sugar

Melt butter in heavy large skillet over medium-high heat. Add apples and sauté until tender, about 5 minutes. Sprinkle with sugar and continue cooking until apples are golden brown.

Champagne Sausage with Sauce Piquante

Leftover Champagne? This is the dish. Form into patties or use casings.

4 servings (about ten 5-inch sausages)

¾ pound trimmed pork shoulder or loin, cut into ½ × 1¾-inch strips
¾ pound trimmed beef chuck or round, cut into ½ × 1¾-inch strips
½ pound trimmed pork fat, cut into ½ × 1¾-inch strips
2 medium garlic cloves
1 large shallot
1½ teaspoons minced fresh marjoram or ½ teaspoon dried, crumbled
½ teaspoon paprika
⅛ teaspoon ground cloves
2 teaspoons salt

¼ teaspoon coarsely ground pepper
¼ cup walnuts (optional), coarsely chopped
⅓ cup (5⅓ tablespoons) brut Champagne or dry red wine

2½ quarts water

1 tablespoon butter
1 tablespoon oil

Sauce Piquante (see following recipe)
Mousselines of Potato, Onion and Garlic (see recipe, p. 16)
Fresh tarragon sprigs (garnish)

If using casings, rinse and soak in tepid water for 1 hour. Freeze pork, beef and fat for 30 minutes, then grind through fine blade of grinder with garlic and shallot. Mix in marjoram, paprika, cloves, salt, pepper and walnuts. Stir in Champagne 1 tablespoon at a time. Cover and refrigerate for 1 hour.

Form sausage mixture into patties or stuff into casings and tie or twist into 10 links. Hang in cool spot until dry or refrigerate on rack, turning occasionally, for 12 to 24 hours.

To cook links: Bring water to simmer in Dutch oven or large saucepan. Add sausages, cover and poach gently until cooked through, 20 minutes. Remove sausages; prick with fork.

To cook patties: Melt butter with oil in heavy large skillet over medium-high heat. Add sausages in batches and fry on both sides until browned and cooked through. Drain on paper towels.

To serve: Spoon Sauce Piquante in center of 4 heated plates. Place Mousselines of Potato, Onion and Garlic at top of each plate and arrange sausage on each side. Garnish with tarragon sprigs.

Sauce Piquante

This sauce can be made a day ahead.

2 cups rich beef stock
½ cup brut Champagne or Madeira
¼ cup tarragon vinegar
1 large shallot, minced
2 tablespoons Cognac
2 tablespoons minced cornichons
2 tablespoons minced capers
Salt and freshly ground pepper

1½ tablespoons minced fresh parsley
1½ tablespoons minced fresh tarragon or 1¼ teaspoons dried, crumbled
1½ tablespoons minced fresh chervil (optional)
2 tablespoons (¼ stick) butter

Boil stock, Champagne, vinegar and shallot in small saucepan until liquid is reduced by half. Stir in Cognac, cornichons, capers, salt and pepper. Just before serving, place over low heat and stir in parsley, tarragon and chervil. Whisk in butter 1 tablespoon at a time, mixing until sauce is slightly thickened.

Italian Sausage

Fennel, the intriguing anise flavor behind the Italian sausage's success, can be echoed in the compatible gnocchi gratin. If fresh fennel is out of season, substitute endive spiked with several tablespoons of pastis (anise liqueur).

4 servings (about nine 5- to 6-inch sausages)

1½ pounds trimmed pork shoulder or loin, cut into ½ × 1¾-inch strips
½ pound trimmed pork fat, cut into ½ × 1¾-inch strips
2¼ teaspoons fennel seed
1 to 3 dried small red chili peppers
1½ teaspoons minced fresh marjoram or ½ teaspoon dried, crumbled
Scant ½ teaspoon whole black peppercorns

½ teaspoon minced garlic
¼ teaspoon paprika
2 teaspoons salt
⅓ cup (5⅓ tablespoons) dry red wine

2½ quarts water
1 tablespoon butter
1 tablespoon oil
Potato Gnocchi and Fennel Gratin (see recipe, page 86)

Rinse sausage casings and soak in tepid water for 1 hour. Freeze pork and fat for 30 minutes, then grind through fine blade of grinder.

Coarsely crush fennel, chilies, marjoram and peppercorns in mortar. Stir into meat with garlic, paprika and salt. Stir in wine 1 tablespoon at a time. Cover and refrigerate 1 hour.

Stuff sausage mixture into casings. Tie or twist into 9 links. Hang in cool spot until dry or refrigerate on a rack, turning occasionally, 12 to 24 hours.

To cook: Bring water to simmer in Dutch oven or large saucepan. Add sausages, cover and poach gently 15 minutes. Drain sausages well, discarding poaching liquid. Pat sausages dry. Heat butter and oil in same saucepan. Add sausages and sauté over medium heat until brown. Serve with Potato Gnocchi and Fennel Gratin.

Chorizo

Complete the Mexican theme with Potato Corn Pancakes and Chile Salsa.

4 to 6 servings (about 8 sausages)

1½ pounds trimmed pork shoulder or loin, cut into ½ × 1¾-inch strips
½ pound trimmed pork fat, cut into ½ × 1¾-inch strips
½ small onion, sliced
2 medium garlic cloves

5 small dried red chili peppers
3 cloves
¾ teaspoon coriander seed
¾ teaspoon cumin seed
2 teaspoons salt
¾ teaspoon paprika

½ teaspoon dried oregano leaves, crumbled
⅛ teaspoon ground red pepper
⅛ teaspoon cinnamon
2 tablespoons Sherry wine vinegar or red wine vinegar

2½ quarts water
1 tablespoon butter
1 tablespoon olive oil
Potato Corn Pancakes and Chile Salsa (see recipe, page 57)

Rinse sausage casings and soak in tepid water for 1 hour. Freeze pork and fat 30 minutes, then grind fat through fine blade of grinder and pork through coarse blade with onion and garlic.

Toast chilies, cloves, coriander and cumin seeds in heavy small skillet over medium-low heat, stirring frequently. Crush coarsely in mortar. Stir into meat with salt, paprika, oregano, red pepper and cinnamon. Stir in vinegar 1 tablespoon at a time. Cover and chill.

Stuff sausage mixture into casings. Tie or twist into 8 links 5 to 6 inches long. Hang in cool spot until dry or refrigerate on a rack, turning occasionally, for about 12 to 24 hours.

To cook: Bring water to simmer in Dutch oven or large saucepan. Add sausages, cover and poach gently 15 minutes. Drain sausages well, discarding poaching liquid. Pat sausages dry. Heat butter and oil in same saucepan over medium heat. Add sausages and sauté until browned on all sides. Serve immediately with pancakes and salsa.

Bockwurst

This mildly seasoned sausage is complemented with an unusual vegetable chartreuse, a mold traditionally assembled to show off the summer's bounty. Our version boasts of winter's comforting flavors with cabbage, leek, bacon and a potato turnip puree. Mustard Wine Sauce blends with both.

4 servings (about 8 sausages)

¾ pound trimmed pork shoulder or loin, cut into ½ × 1¾-inch strips
¾ pound veal shoulder or breast, cut into ½ × 1¾-inch strips
½ pound trimmed pork fat, cut into ½ × 1¾-inch strips
1½ tablespoons minced chives
¾ teaspoon paprika
½ teaspoon ground ginger
¼ teaspoon ground cardamom
¼ teaspoon freshly grated nutmeg

⅛ teaspoon cinnamon
2 teaspoons salt
¼ teaspoon freshly ground pepper
3 tablespoons whipping cream, milk or dry white wine

2½ quarts veal stock or water

Chartreuse of Winter Vegetables (see recipe, page 87)
Mustard Wine Sauce (see following recipe)

Rinse sausage casings and soak in tepid water for 1 hour. Freeze pork, veal and fat for 30 minutes, then grind through fine blade of grinder. Mix in chives, paprika, ginger, cardamom, nutmeg, cinnamon, salt and pepper. Stir in cream 1 tablespoon at a time. Cover and refrigerate for 1 hour.

Stuff sausage mixture into casings. Tie or twist into 8 links. Hang in cool spot until dry or refrigerate on rack, turning occasionally, 12 to 24 hours.

To cook: Bring stock to simmer in Dutch oven or large saucepan. Add sausages, cover and poach gently until cooked through, about 20 minutes.

To serve: Unmold Chartreuse of Winter Vegetables onto heated serving platter. Arrange sausages around edge. Serve with Mustard Wine Sauce.

Mustard Wine Sauce

This sauce can be made a day ahead.

Makes about 1¾ cups

2½ cups rich veal or beef stock
½ cup red wine
¼ cup white wine vinegar
1 tablespoon coarse stoneground mustard

Salt and freshly ground pepper
1 tablespoon minced chives
2 tablespoons (¼ stick) butter

Boil stock, wine and vinegar in small saucepan until reduced by half. Stir in mustard, salt and pepper. Just before serving, place over low heat and stir in chives. Whisk in butter 1 tablespoon at a time, mixing until butter is melted and sauce is smooth.

❧ General Directions for Sausage Making and Cooking

The Mixture

1. Trim meat and fat of all gristle and connective tissue.

2. Cut meat into long, narrow strips; freeze for 30 minutes before grinding.

3. In an electric grinder, allow fat and meat to feed through with very little assistance from the wooden tamper.

4. Grind a bit of fat first to grease the grinder; finish grinding with a piece of bread to remove last bits of meat.

5. After mixture is ground, stir it over ice or refrigerate it for an hour to make it easier to handle.

The Casing

1. You will need about two yards of casing for each of the following recipes.

2. Wash casing to rid it of salt by slipping one end over the faucet and running warm water through it.

3. Cut into manageable lengths—about two feet. If there are holes in casing, tie them closed or cut them off.

4. Soak in tepid water for one hour.

5. Wring out the casing before filling it.

Filling the Casing

1. Attach stuffing horn to grinder.

2. Place one end of prepared casing over the horn. Gradually push all of casing onto the horn, leaving a 2-inch overlap below the horn. Tie a knot in this overlapping end.

3. With your right hand, feed ground mixture into grinder a bit at a time.

4. Anchor casing on top of the horn with your left thumb, allowing casing to unroll as mixture is extruded.

5. Stop filling process occasionally to mold meat into casing. Pierce any air bubbles with a needle.

6. Do not pack too full or it will burst as the filling expands during cooking.

Saucisson en Croute (Sausage in Pastry)

8 servings

Filling
- 1 pound good quality pork sausage
- 1 bunch green onions (including tops), chopped
- ½ pound mushrooms (about 4 large), coarsely chopped
- 3 to 4 garlic cloves, minced
- 2 eggs, lightly beaten
- ½ cup fresh breadcrumbs
- 1 tablespoon whole mustard seed
- ½ teaspoon ground red pepper
- Salt

7. After casing has been filled, remove it—with the horn still attached to one end—from machine.

8. Push any remaining sausage through horn with a spoon handle.

9. Take off horn and knot casing.

10. Leftover casing can be repacked with coarse salt and refrigerated.

Dividing into Links

1. Knot 3-inch pieces of string around sausage at equally spaced intervals, or twist one measured link clockwise and the next one counterclockwise so they don't unwind.

2. For individual sausages, compress meat so there is ½ inch of empty casing between links. Tie a knot at each end of the space and cut between.

3. Divide and cut sausages as you go.

4. The tighter sausages are tied, the more they curve.

Drying

To develop their flavor, hang sausages to dry for 12 to 24 hours on a hanger or pasta rack in a cool spot. They can also be dried on rack in refrigerator.

Cooking

1. Sausages are toughened and dried out by overcooking. For juiciest presentation, poach them gently in water, stock, wine or beer.

2. Test for doneness when a sample slice reveals they are brown through, or a meat thermometer reads 165°F or their juices run clear when pricked.

Keeping

1. To keep leftover sausages plump, place them in cold water while they are still warm. Let cool in water.

2. Uncooked sausages will keep for three days in the refrigerator or up to three months in the freezer.

Puff Pastry

1 1-pound package (2 prerolled sheets) frozen puff pastry dough   ¼ cup (½ stick) butter, melted

For filling: Cook sausage in medium skillet over medium heat, stirring and breaking up with fork until browned, about 5 minutes. Drain well. Transfer to bowl. Add remaining ingredients for filling and blend well. Set aside.

For pastry: Preheat oven to 425°F. Roll out each sheet on lightly floured surface to thickness of ⅛ inch and length of about 12 inches. Spread filling over lower third of long edge. Roll up jelly roll fashion, tucking in ends. Bake, basting occasionally with butter, until golden brown, about 45 minutes.

Schnitzen (Bacon with Dried Fruits and Potatoes)

6 to 8 servings

5 ounces dried pears	10 ounces lean bacon, thickly sliced*
5 ounces dried apples	1 to 2 cups meat stock
¼ cup sugar	1½ pounds potatoes
2 tablespoons water	Salt and freshly ground pepper

Soak pears and apples overnight in enough water to cover. Drain well.

Combine sugar and water in small saucepan. Cover and boil until syrup begins to turn golden brown, shaking pan several times. Remove from heat and add fruit, turning to coat all surfaces. Place bacon in Dutch oven or large pot. Arrange fruit over top. Dissolve any caramel remaining in pan with small amount of meat stock and add to fruit. Cover and simmer until bacon and fruit are almost tender, about 35 to 45 minutes.

Peel and quarter potatoes. Add to pot and sprinkle with salt and pepper. Cover and cook until potatoes are tender, about 30 minutes, adding more stock as necessary (mixture should be moist but not soupy).

For a variation, add a smoked Strasbourg sausage weighing about ½ pound to the potatoes.

*Lean slab bacon can be used in place of slices. Remove before serving.

Glazed Ham Loaf

Team this delicious loaf with eggs fixed "sunny-side up" or with the German Apple Pancake (see recipe, page 52). For lunch or a light supper, any leftover ham can be used to perk up an omelet or as a filling for pita bread.

8 to 10 servings

Glaze

1¼ cups lightly packed dark brown sugar	½ pound fresh pork, ground
¼ cup tarragon vinegar	1 cup parsley leaves, minced
2 tablespoons Madeira wine	⅔ cup milk
2 teaspoons dry mustard	1 egg
	4 small shallots, minced
Ham Loaf	2 tablespoons Glaze
2 pounds cooked ham, finely chopped	1 teaspoon dried thyme
	½ teaspoon freshly grated nutmeg
	Freshly ground pepper

Preheat oven to 450°F.

For glaze: Combine all ingredients in food processor or blender. Remove and set aside.

For ham loaf: Combine all ingredients in mixing bowl and blend uniformly using wooden spoon or your hands. Turn mixture into 9 × 13-inch baking dish and shape into oval loaf. Brush generously with glaze. Bake 20 minutes. Reduce heat to 300°F and bake an additional 45 minutes, basting several times with additional glaze. Remove from oven, drain off juices and brush generously with remaining glaze. May be served hot or cold. (Can be very thinly sliced if chilled.)

3 ❧ Pancakes, Breads and Pastries

Next to freshly brewed coffee, there is probably no more welcome aroma in the morning than that of dough baking or batter cooking. If you have ever dreamed of living in Paris above a *boulangerie* or *pâtisserie*, the recipes in this chapter provide the next best thing: a chance to create your own bakery or pastry shop (or pancake house, for that matter) right at home.

Sweet pancakes and their close relatives surely rank with the all-time favorites for breakfast and brunch. And among the recipes that follow, you'll find pancakes for every taste—buttermilk, sourdough and puffy versions; pancakes flavored with orange or apples; even crepes with a chocolate topping. Or you might try Orange Nut Waffles with Orange Syrup (page 54) or French Toast with Apple Custard Sauce (page 55).

When your sweet tooth is on vacation, there are savory pancakes and crepes. We offer several kinds of delicate vegetable pancakes; corn pancakes from Mexico, perfect with green chili salsa; a foolproof crepe batter with variations; and, if you are feeling particularly festive, Buckwheat Blini (page 61), to be served in the Russian style with caviar, smoked salmon and sour cream.

Muffins and other quick breads offer a cozy, nostalgic feeling and great taste with very little effort. Try any of these recipes for coffee cakes, old-fashioned blueberry buckle, bonnach from Scotland, other flavored loaves, and a selection of muffins—bran, corn bran, and an unusual rice-raisin version. Yeast breads and cakes take a little more time—the yeast has to do its work—but the English muffins, brioches, savarins, kugel-hupfs, and a collection of special holiday breads from different countries are well worth the extra effort.

The pastry-maker's glories—croissants, Danish pastries and strudels, are almost as impressive to look at as they are good to eat. And from a few basic doughs you can fill a pastry cart with buttery, flaky delicacies in all shapes, sizes and flavors.

A big plus in all these recipes is that they are not daunting; any home cook can make them, and have a good time doing it. The only hard part is making a choice. . . .

Sweet Pancakes, Waffles and Toasts

The Magnolia Hotel's Puffy Pancakes

4 servings

6 eggs
1 cup all purpose flour
1 cup milk
½ cup sugar
¼ cup frozen orange juice
concentrate

1 tablespoon butter

4 tablespoons (½ stick) butter
Lemon wedges (garnish)
Powdered sugar (garnish)
Sweetened fresh berries (garnish)

Combine eggs, flour, milk, sugar and orange juice in processor or blender and mix well. Add 1 tablespoon butter and blend in thoroughly.

Preheat oven to 450°F. Add 1 tablespoon butter to each of four 1-cup oval or round baking dishes. Heat dishes in oven until butter is melted but not browned. Divide batter evenly among dishes. Bake until puffed and golden, about 20 minutes. Serve immediately with lemon wedges, powdered sugar and fresh berries.

Sourdough Pancakes

Makes about twelve 4-inch pancakes

1 cup all purpose flour
1 cup buttermilk, heated to 100°F
¼ cup Basic Sourdough Starter (see following recipe), room temperature

2 tablespoons sour cream

½ teaspoon baking soda
1 egg, beaten
2 tablespoons oil
1 tablespoon sugar
¼ teaspoon salt

Combine flour, buttermilk and starter in medium bowl and blend well. Cover and refrigerate overnight.

Mix sour cream with baking soda and blend into buttermilk mixture. Stir in remaining ingredients, blending thoroughly. Let stand 10 minutes.

Meanwhile, preheat griddle to 325°F; grease lightly. Drop batter by spoonfuls onto griddle and cook until browned on both sides, turning once.

Basic Sourdough Starter

Makes about 1½ cups

1 cup lukewarm purified water
(90°F to 105°F)
⅓ cup instant nonfat dry milk

3 tablespoons lowfat plain yogurt

1 cup all purpose flour

Rinse 1½- to 2-quart glass or ceramic bowl with hot water several minutes and wipe dry. Combine water and dry milk in bowl, stirring until milk is dissolved. Blend in yogurt. Cover with plastic wrap and let stand in warm draft-free area until consistency of yogurt, about 12 to 24 hours.

Using plastic spoon, gradually add flour, blending until smooth. Cover and let stand in warm draft-free area until mixture is full of bubbles and has sour aroma, about 2 to 4 days. The starter is now ready to use. Store covered in refrigerator in plastic or ceramic container (do not use glass).

Sweet Crepes with Chocolate Topping

Makes about 2 dozen crepes (8 to 12 servings)

Crepes
- 1 cup all purpose flour
- 2 tablespoons sugar
- 3 eggs
- 2 egg yolks
- 1¾ cups plus 2 tablespoons milk
- 2 tablespoons Cognac or brandy
- 1 tablespoon finely grated orange or lemon peel

Pinch of salt

Topping
- 4 ounces semisweet chocolate, grated
- 1 tablespoon sugar
- 2 tablespoons (¼ stick) unsalted butter, cut into pieces

For crepes: Combine flour and sugar in large bowl. Make well in center. Add eggs, yolks and ½ cup milk to bowl, whisking flour in slowly until mixture is smooth and shiny. Gradually whisk in remaining milk with Cognac. Stir in peel and salt. Let rest at room temperature about 2 hours. *(Batter can be prepared 2 days ahead and refrigerated.)*

To cook crepes, follow instructions for Savory Crepes (see recipe, page 58).

To assemble: Preheat oven to 350°F. Generously butter large round or square baking dish. Fold each crepe in half and then in half again to form triangle. Arrange in single layer in prepared dish, overlapping slightly. Sprinkle with chocolate and sugar. Dot with butter. Bake until chocolate is melted and crepes are heated through, about 20 minutes. Serve hot.

Variations

Apple Crepes: Fill Sweet Crepes with apple puree or sautéed apples. Roll up cigar fashion and arrange seam side down in greased flameproof baking dish. Sprinkle with sugar and run under broiler until caramelized.

Chocolate Crepes: Prepare batter for Sweet Crepes in processor or blender, substituting ¼ cup unsweetened cocoa powder for ¼ cup of flour. Use rum, coffee liqueur or crème de cacao instead of Cognac. Fill with chocolate mousse, bavarian cream or soufflé. Top with powdered sugar and whipped cream. (Chocolate crepes should be made thicker than standard recipe.)

Nut Crepes: Prepare batter for Sweet Crepes, reducing flour by 2 tablespoons and adding ½ cup ground nuts. Fill with nut custard. Serve warm with a rich chocolate sauce.

Quick Scandinavian Pancake

This easy variation of the classic French crepe can be served with butter, syrup or cinnamon-sugar for breakfast or stuffed with meat or vegetables.

Makes 1 pancake (do not double recipe)

- 1 egg
- 1 tablespoon water
- 1 tablespoon oil
- 1 tablespoon whole wheat flour
- 2 to 3 tablespoons oil

Preheat oven to 200°F. Combine first 4 ingredients in small bowl and whisk thoroughly. Heat remaining oil in 10-inch skillet over medium-high heat. Pour batter into skillet, rotating pan until thinly covered. Cook until golden, about 1 minute. Turn pancake over and continue cooking until golden, about 1 minute. Stack pancakes on plate and keep warm in oven until ready to serve.

🍎 Sourdough: Start Your Own

Sourdough is a leavening agent and, like yeast, it is a living thing. Properly cared for, a starter made from sourdough will live for years. By following the basic recipe below, you can raise your own sourdough starter and use it to turn out everything from bread and English muffins to pancakes and coffee cake—all with the zesty tart flavor and distinctive chewy texture of sourdough.

Temperature is probably the most important factor in the art of sourdough. In too cold an environment the starter will not thrive and bubble; too hot and the all-important bacteria are killed. Water for the starter must be heated to between 90°F and 105°F and the initial mixture left to stand in a draft-free area that maintains a temperature of between 80°F and 90°F. The places that usually work the best are a gas oven with pilot light (set container near it, not *over* it), the top of a refrigerator, dryer or indoor water heater or inside a warm cupboard. An electric oven can also be used if you place a small votive candle in a bottom corner of it. Place the starter on a rack in the upper third of the oven.

After 12 to 14 hours, the initial mixture will be curdy and have the consistency of yogurt. Any clear liquid that rises to the surface during this time can simply be stirred back in (use a wooden or plastic spoon, never metal). But if a thin pink liquid comes to the top, you will have to discard this mixture and begin again.

Once the mixture has thickened, a small amount of flour is added. This is the starter, which is then covered and left in that same warm environment for up to four days to sour. Once the starter comes "alive," is full of bubbles

German Apple Pancake

Makes 2 large pancakes (6 to 8 servings)

Batter
- 8 extra-large eggs
- 1 cup unbleached all purpose flour (5 ounces)
- 2 tablespoons sugar
- 1 teaspoon baking powder
- ⅛ teaspoon salt
- 2 cups milk
- ¼ cup (½ stick) butter, melted
- 2 teaspoons vanilla
- ¼ teaspoon freshly grated nutmeg

Fruit Mixture
- ½ cup (1 stick) unsalted butter
- 1⅓ cups sugar (9½ ounces)
- 1 teaspoon cinnamon
- ¼ teaspoon freshly grated nutmeg
- 2 large tart apples (Granny Smith or greening), peeled, halved, cored and thinly sliced (2 cups)

For batter: Combine first 6 ingredients in mixing bowl and blend with spoon or electric mixer until smooth. Add melted butter, vanilla and nutmeg and blend. Let batter stand at room temperature for 30 minutes or in refrigerator overnight.

For fruit mixture: Position rack in center of oven and preheat to 425°F. Divide butter evenly and melt in two 10-inch ovenproof skillets, brushing butter up sides of pan. Remove from heat. Combine sugar, cinnamon and nutmeg and blend well. Sprinkle ⅓ cup over butter in each skillet. Divide apple slices and layer evenly over butter. Sprinkle remaining sugar mixture over apples.

Place skillets over medium-high heat only until mixture bubbles. Divide batter evenly and gently pour over apples. Transfer skillets to oven and bake pancakes 15 minutes. Reduce heat to 375°F and bake an additional 10 minutes. Slide onto heated serving platters, cut into wedges and serve immediately.

and has a great sour, earthy aroma, it is ready to use. Store it covered in the refrigerator in a plastic or ceramic container. Do not use glass for storage since the gases produced during fermentation may crack or shatter it. Always remember to bring starter to room temperature before using it.

The bacteria essential for fermentation of a sourdough starter are present in many foods. Our version uses a combination of lowfat plain yogurt, warm water and nonfat dry milk to which flour is then added, resulting in a particularly active starter. Each time the starter is used it must be replenished with equal amounts of flour and the milk powder-warm water mixture. For instance, if you use ½ cup of starter, "feed" the remainder by adding ½ cup all purpose flour and ½ cup lukewarm water (90°F to 105°F) mixed with about 2½ tablespoons instant nonfat dry milk. Cover and let stand in a warm draft-free area until the mixture is bubbly once again, then store covered in the refrigerator for several days before using (this will allow the starter to reactivate). Actually, the starter must be replenished after two weeks whether it has been used or not. Simply discard ½ cup and feed as directed above.

Few people realize that freshly fed starter can be frozen up to 2 months—ideal for those who want starter on hand but do not bake regularly. Freezing slows the fermentation process. When ready to use, let starter thaw at room temperature and then let stand in a warm draft-free area until bubbly.

Naturally, the longer you keep a starter going the more sour (and better!) it will get. Instead of discarding that ½ cup before replenishing, you might try passing it along to friends and relatives.

A Russian Grandma's Cheese Blintzes

Makes 24 to 26 blintzes

Crepes
4 eggs
2 cups water
¼ cup milk
2 tablespoons (¼ stick) butter
1¾ cups all purpose flour

Filling
2 cups cottage cheese
8 ounces farmer cheese

6 ounces cream cheese
6 tablespoons sugar
1 egg
1½ teaspoons vanilla
½ cup raisins (optional)

2 tablespoons (¼ stick) butter
Fresh strawberries (garnish)
Strawberry Yogurt Sauce (see
following recipe)

For crepes: Place eggs, water and milk in blender, processor or bowl. Melt butter in 6-inch skillet; remove from heat. Blend egg mixture. Add melted butter and flour and mix until smooth. Refrigerate 1 to 2 hours. Lightly wipe skillet with paper towel and set aside.

Heat skillet until drop of water bounces off surface. Add scant ¼ cup crepe batter and tilt pan quickly to cover entire surface; pour out any excess batter. Cook over medium heat until edges of crepe begin to curl and brown; *do not turn.* Place crepe browned side up on towel and cover lightly. Repeat with remaining batter. Keep covered until ready to fill and form into blintzes.

For filling: Combine cheeses, sugar, egg and vanilla in bowl or processor and blend well. Stir in raisins if desired.

Spoon 1 heaping tablespoon filling down center of crepe. Tuck two sides toward center, then fold in remaining two sides to enclose like an envelope. Place seam side down on platter. Repeat with remaining crepes and filling.

Heat 2 tablespoons butter until hot and bubbly in large skillet. Add blintzes seam side down and fry until golden brown on both sides. Transfer to heated plates. Garnish with strawberries and serve with Strawberry Yogurt Sauce.

Strawberry Yogurt Sauce

2 cups plain yogurt	¼ cup sugar
1 cup hulled strawberries	½ teaspoon finely grated lemon peel

Combine 1 cup yogurt with remaining ingredients in blender or processor and mix 30 seconds. Stir in remaining yogurt with spoon. Refrigerate for at least 1 hour before serving.

Oat Waffles

Makes about 4 to 6 waffles

2 eggs, separated	1 tablespoon honey or brown sugar
1 cup warm water	1½ cups Oat-Wheat Germ Breakfast Mix (see following recipe)
¼ cup oil	

Preheat waffle iron. Beat yolks with water, oil and honey or sugar. Stir in mix only until ingredients are moistened. Beat egg whites until stiff. Fold into batter. Spoon onto waffle iron and cook to desired doneness.

Oat-Wheat Germ Breakfast Mix

Makes about 9 cups

3 cups quick-cooking oats	2 teaspoons salt
2 cups unbleached flour	½ teaspoon cream of tartar
2 cups whole wheat flour	2 cups (4 sticks) butter or
1 cup raw wheat germ	margarine (or combination),
1 cup dry milk powder	slightly softened
3 tablespoons baking powder	

Combine first 8 ingredients and blend well. Cut in butter and/or margarine with pastry blender or knives until mixture resembles coarse meal. Store tightly covered in refrigerator.

Orange Nut Waffles with Orange Syrup

2 servings

1½ cups cake flour	1 tablespoon finely grated orange peel
3 tablespoons sugar	½ cup finely chopped walnuts
2½ teaspoons baking powder	6 tablespoons melted butter
½ teaspoon salt	Orange Syrup (see following recipe)
2 eggs, separated	
½ cup milk	
½ cup freshly squeezed orange juice, strained	

Preheat waffle iron. Sift flour, sugar, baking powder and salt into small bowl. Beat egg yolks in medium bowl until thickened. Add milk, orange juice and orange peel and mix thoroughly. Gradually add flour mixture, blending well. Stir in walnuts and butter. Beat egg whites in small bowl until stiff. Fold into walnut mixture. Bake waffles in waffle iron according to manufacturer's instructions. Serve immediately with Orange Syrup.

Orange Syrup

Makes about 1⅔ cups

1 cup sugar
⅔ cup freshly squeezed orange juice
2 tablespoons dark rum

1 tablespoon curaçao
Coarsely grated peel of 1 orange

Combine sugar and orange juice in small saucepan and bring to boil over low heat, stirring constantly. Remove from heat. Blend in remaining ingredients. Let cool completely. Strain into jar with tight-fitting lid. Refrigerate. Reheat syrup before serving.

French Toast with Apple Custard Sauce

6 servings

Oil
4 eggs
1 cup whipping cream
¼ teaspoon salt
3 large thick slices egg bread (crusts trimmed), cut diagonally into 6 triangles

Powdered sugar
Apple Custard Sauce (see following recipe)

Heat ½ inch oil in electric skillet to 325°F. Preheat oven to 400°F. Beat eggs, cream and salt in medium bowl. Dip each slice of bread, allowing it to soak up as much liquid as possible. Fry in hot oil until browned, turning only once. Transfer to baking sheet and bake until puffed, about 3 to 5 minutes. Drain on paper towels. Arrange on heated platter, sprinkle with powdered sugar and serve immediately with Apple Custard Sauce on the side.

Apple Custard Sauce

1 cup milk
2 eggs
2 tablespoons sugar
1 teaspoon vanilla

Pinch of salt
½ cup applesauce
1 teaspoon minced lemon zest

Heat milk in top of double boiler over gently simmering water until small bubbles form around edge. Combine eggs, sugar, vanilla and salt in mixing bowl and beat well. Slowly whisk milk into egg mixture, beating constantly until well blended. Return to double boiler and continue cooking over low heat until sauce is thickened. Stir in applesauce and zest and heat through.

Superduper French Toast

4 servings

6 eggs
⅔ cup orange juice
⅓ cup Grand Marnier
⅓ cup milk
3 tablespoons sugar
¼ teaspoon vanilla
¼ teaspoon salt

Finely grated peel of 1 orange
8 ¾-inch-thick slices French bread

3 to 4 tablespoons butter
Powdered sugar
Butter
Maple syrup

Beat eggs in large bowl. Add orange juice, Grand Marnier, milk, sugar, vanilla, salt and peel and mix well. Dip bread into egg mixture, turning to coat all surfaces. Transfer to baking dish in single layer. Pour any remaining egg mixture over top;

cover and refrigerate overnight, turning occasionally (liquid will be absorbed).

Melt butter in large skillet over medium-high heat. Add bread slices in batches and cook until browned, about 8 minutes. Turn and continue cooking until browned, about 8 minutes. Cut bread diagonally. Arrange on platter and sprinkle with powdered sugar. Serve immediately. Pass butter and maple syrup.

Savory Pancakes and Crepes

Italian Rice Pancakes with Spinach Basil Sauce

Makes about sixteen 2-inch pancakes

4 ounces mushrooms, sliced (about 10 medium)

2 tablespoons (¼ stick) butter
3 tablespoons minced onion
½ cup Italian Arborio rice
1 to 1½ cups simmering chicken stock
1 tablespoon all purpose flour
2 eggs (room temperature), separated
1½ ounces (about 6 tablespoons) freshly grated Parmesan cheese

Pinch of salt
Pinch of cream of tartar
Salt and freshly ground pepper

2 tablespoons clarified butter (or more) or 1 tablespoon butter and 1 tablespoon oil
Spinach Basil Sauce (see following recipe)
2 tablespoons freshly grated Parmesan cheese

Toasted pine nuts (garnish)

Combine mushrooms with enough water to cover in heavy small saucepan. Cover, place over medium-high heat and bring to boil. Reduce heat and simmer 2 minutes. Remove saucepan from heat and set aside, covered.

Melt butter in heavy small saucepan over very low heat. Add onion, cover and cook 10 minutes. Stir in rice. Increase heat to medium, pour in ½ cup simmering stock and stir until stock is absorbed. Repeat with as much of remaining stock as necessary until rice is tender and creamy, stirring constantly, about 30 minutes. Remove mushrooms from poaching liquid using slotted spoon. Stir into rice. Cool at least 15 minutes. Boil mushroom poaching liquid over medium-high heat until reduced to 2 tablespoons. Set aside for Spinach Basil Sauce. Stir flour, egg yolks and 1½ ounces Parmesan into rice. Beat egg whites in large bowl until foamy. Add pinch of salt and cream of tartar and continue beating until whites are stiff but not dry. Gently stir ¼ of whites into rice mixture, then fold rice mixture into remaining whites. Season with salt and pepper.

Melt clarified butter on griddle or in heavy skillet over medium heat. Ladle 2-inch pancakes onto griddle; do not crowd. Cook until bottom is medium brown, 2 to 3 minutes. Turn and brown second side (pancakes are fragile and are easier to turn if sandwiched between 2 spatulas). Repeat with remaining batter, adding more butter to griddle as necessary. As pancakes are finished, arrange in single layer on ungreased baking sheet or in gratin dish. Top with warm Spinach Basil Sauce. Sprinkle with 2 tablespoons Parmesan. *(Can be prepared several hours ahead to this point and kept at room temperature.)*

Preheat broiler. Broil pancakes briefly until cheese is melted and golden brown. Garnish with toasted pine nuts and serve immediately.

Spinach Basil Sauce

Makes about 1 cup

1 large bunch (about 1 pound) fresh spinach, stemmed and rinsed (do not dry)

2 tablespoons (¼ stick) butter
1 cup whipping cream
Reserved mushroom poaching liquid (see preceding recipe)

1 egg yolk
1 to 2 tablespoons minced fresh basil
Salt and freshly ground pepper
1 tablespoon fresh lemon juice
⅛ teaspoon freshly grated nutmeg

Place large casserole or Dutch oven over medium-high heat. Gradually add spinach, stirring until wilted. Reduce heat to low and cook just until tender, 2 to 3 minutes. Rinse spinach under cold running water and squeeze dry; chop coarsely.

Melt butter in saucepan over medium heat. Add spinach, ½ cup cream and reserved mushroom poaching liquid. Cook until liquid is absorbed, stirring occasionally, about 8 minutes. Mix egg yolk with remaining cream. Reduce heat to low, add yolk mixture to spinach and cook, stirring, until thickened, about 3 minutes. Season with basil, salt and pepper. Blend in lemon juice and nutmeg and set aside. Just before serving, stir over low heat to rewarm; do not boil or sauce will curdle.

Potato Corn Pancakes and Chile Salsa

4 servings

2 tablespoons (¼ stick) butter
12 ounces fresh poblano chilies (also called pasilla and ancho), roasted, peeled, seeded and coarsely chopped*

2 tablespoons all purpose flour
1 teaspoon salt
¼ teaspoon freshly ground pepper
2 eggs, separated and brought to room temperature
¼ cup whipping cream
Kernels from 1 ear of corn

1 pound baking potatoes, peeled and grated
Pinch of salt
Pinch of cream of tartar

2 tablespoons (¼ stick) butter
2 tablespoons oil

Crème fraîche or sour cream (garnish)

Chorizo (see recipe, page 44)

Melt butter in heavy small skillet over low heat. Add chilies, cover and let sweat, stirring occasionally, 10 minutes. Remove from heat and set aside.

Combine flour, salt and pepper in large bowl. Mix egg yolks and cream in small bowl. Gradually stir into flour just until moistened. Stir in corn.

Wash potatoes (to eliminate starch) until water runs clear. Dry thoroughly in salad spinner or towel. Beat egg whites with salt and cream of tartar until stiff but not dry. Add potatoes to corn mixture and blend well. Fold in egg whites. *Use batter immediately or it will become watery.*

Preheat oven to 200°F. Form 3-inch pancakes on griddle or in skillet heated with butter and oil. Fry until bottoms are browned and set, about 5 minutes. Turn and brown second side, pressing pancakes lightly with spatula. To keep warm, arrange in single layer on rack in oven. Repeat with remaining batter, mixing gently before cooking.

To serve: Gently reheat chilies. Arrange pancakes on platter and surround with chorizo. Spoon chilies over sausage. Top with crème fraîche or sour cream.

* Canned chilies can be substituted.

Savory Crepes

The directions that follow are for making the crepe batter by hand. To prepare in the blender, combine all ingredients and mix on high speed until the batter is smooth, about 1 minute. For food processor crepes, mix eggs and dry ingredients in work bowl with several on/off turns. Then, with machine running, pour milk through feed tube and mix well. For best results, have milk and eggs at room temperature for all these methods. A nonstick pan requires less butter for cooking.

Makes about 2 dozen crepes (8 to 12 servings)

1 cup all purpose flour
Pinch of sugar
3 eggs
2 egg yolks
2 cups milk
1 teaspoon salt

¼ teaspoon freshly ground pepper
⅛ teaspoon freshly grated nutmeg

6 tablespoons (¾ stick) unsalted butter

Combine flour and sugar in large bowl. Make well in center. Add eggs, yolks and ½ cup milk to well, whisking flour in slowly until mixture is smooth and shiny. Gradually whisk in remaining milk. Season with salt, pepper and nutmeg. (Press batter through sieve if lumps remain.) Let rest at room temperature about 2 hours. *(Batter can be prepared 2 days ahead and refrigerated.)*

Melt butter in 6½-inch crepe pan. Remove from heat and let cool slightly. Stir half into crepe batter, mixing well. (Batter should be consistency of heavy cream. If too thick, stir in more milk; if too thin, place several tablespoons all purpose flour in another bowl and gradually stir batter into it.) Pour remaining butter in small cup. Skim off foam to clarify.

Heat crepe pan over medium-high heat. Remove from heat and brush with some of clarified butter. Return to heat; sprinkle with small amount of water. If beads "dance" on pan, it is ready. Remove pan from heat. Working quickly, add about 3 tablespoons batter to one edge of pan, tilting and swirling until bottom is covered with thin layer of batter; pour any excess batter back into bowl.

Return pan to medium-high heat. Loosen edges of crepe with small spatula or knife, discarding any pieces of crepe clinging to sides of pan. Cook crepe until bottom is brown. Turn (or flip) crepe over and cook second side until brown. Slide out onto plate. Top with sheet of waxed paper or foil. Repeat with remaining batter, stirring occasionally and adjusting heat and adding more clarified butter to crepe pan or skillet as necessary.

Variations

Green Herb Crepes: Prepare batter for Savory Crepes in processor or blender, increasing milk to 2½ cups. Add 1 bunch cooked, chopped, squeezed-dry spinach and mix well. Blend in 1½ tablespoons *each* minced fresh parsley, chives, chervil and tarragon (or 2 teaspoons each dried, crumbled). Fill with mushroom duxelles or fish.

Cornmeal Beer Crepes: Prepare batter for Savory Crepes, substituting beer for milk. Reduce flour by 2 tablespoons and add ¼ cup cornmeal. Remix in blender after resting time. Excellent filled with sausage.

Nut Crepes: Prepare batter for Savory Crepes, reducing flour by 2 tablespoons and adding ½ cup ground nuts. Fill with chicken or turkey salad.

Mediterranean Crepes: Prepare batter for Savory Crepes, substituting olive oil for 3 tablespoons melted butter added to batter. Heat ½ cup of the milk and add 1 teaspoon crushed saffron threads, stirring until dissolved.

Zucchini-Onion Pancakes Gratinées

Makes about thirty 2½-inch pancakes

¼ cup (½ stick) butter
3 small to medium onions, thinly sliced
2 small zucchini (8 ounces total), thinly sliced

½ cup milk
3 eggs
⅓ cup all purpose flour
½ cup freshly grated Parmesan cheese

⅛ teaspoon freshly grated nutmeg
Salt and freshly ground pepper

2 tablespoons clarified butter (or more) or 1 tablespoon butter and 1 tablespoon oil

⅓ cup whipping cream
½ cup freshly grated Parmesan cheese

Melt butter in heavy large skillet over low heat. Add onion, cover and cook, stirring occasionally, 20 minutes; do not let onion brown. Increase heat to medium, add zucchini and stir until almost tender, 2 to 3 minutes. Set aside at least 20 minutes to cool.

Mix milk, eggs, flour and ½ cup Parmesan in processor or blender. Add zucchini mixture and mince using on/off turns. Blend in nutmeg. Season to taste with salt and pepper.

Melt clarified butter on griddle or in heavy skillet over medium heat. Ladle 2½-inch pancakes onto griddle. Cook until bottom is medium brown, 2 to 3 minutes. Turn and brown second side. Repeat with remaining batter, adding more butter to griddle as necessary. Arrange pancakes in large gratin pan or broilerproof baking dish, overlapping as little as possible. *(Can be prepared several hours ahead to this point and kept at room temperature.)*

Preheat broiler. Pour cream over pancakes and sprinkle evenly with ½ cup Parmesan. Broil until cheese is melted and golden brown. Serve immediately.

Herb Crepes Bernoise

6 servings

2 tablespoons (¼ stick) unsalted butter
½ pound mushrooms, minced
2 tablespoons finely minced green onion (including greens)
Salt and freshly ground white pepper

8 ounces cream cheese, room temperature

2 cups sour cream
3 tablespoons freshly grated Parmesan cheese
2 tablespoons minced fresh dill
12 to 14 Herb Crepes (see following recipe)
6 tablespoons (¾ stick) unsalted butter, melted

Preheat oven to 325°F. Butter large shallow baking dish. Melt 2 tablespoons butter in 10-inch skillet over medium heat. Add mushrooms and green onion and cook until liquid has evaporated. Season with salt and pepper to taste and set aside.

Combine cream cheese and sour cream in large mixing bowl and mash with fork. Add mushroom mixture, Parmesan and dill and mix well. Taste and adjust seasoning. Divide mixture evenly among crepes. Roll up cigar fashion and place seam side down in baking dish. Pour butter over top. Bake until heated through, about 20 minutes.

❦ *Crepes*

Crepes—those simple pancakes of flour, milk, eggs and seasonings—offer almost limitless possibilities for any meal. The French have been singing their praises for centuries. Italians do a variation on the theme with cannelloni, the Chinese with egg rolls, Mexicans with tortillas. In fact, almost every culture has found a place for the versatile crepe in its repertoire.

Once you have mastered the easy crepe-making technique, you will have the savory or sweet basis for a delicious first course, main course or dessert. They can be simmered in a sauce, filled or layered with a delectable stuffing or soufflé, or flamed in liqueur. Press them into service to wrap croquettes, garnish consommé or line a mold. Crepes are as inexpensive as rice, dumplings or noodles, and are even better for dressing up your leftovers.

The pan selected for crepe preparation will determine whether the operation is a breeze or a struggle. The French cast-iron crepe pan, with its long handle and low sloping sides that facilitate flipping, is an excellent conductor of heat. This classic must be seasoned before it is used by filling it with vegetable oil and baking in a 200°F oven for four hours. As long as it is not washed or used for anything else, it will build up an excellent nonstick surface. To clean, sprinkle the pan with coarse salt and a bit of oil and wipe with a paper towel. Another popular pan is the 6½-inch heavy-duty aluminum skillet with a handle that does not get hot. Small nonstick skillets also work well. Omelet pans can also be used, but the shape is not as practical.

Once the crepes are prepared, the ways to fill them are infinite. But to get you started, here is a sampling of some of the combinations: sautéed chicken livers; oyster and spinach; mushroom and ham or chicken; or zucchini, eggplant, tomato, onions and roasted peppers. Nap with Mornay sauce before baking. Other possibilities include shrimp- or mixed seafood-filled crepes with tomato or spaghetti sauce.

Crepes are also a great idea for informal parties. Prepare a quantity of crepes, arrange them on a buffet with a variety of fillings and toppings and let guests assemble their own. And the bonus for the busy cook? Crepes are ideal do-ahead fare. Stack the freshly cooked crepes between sheets of waxed paper or foil and cool. Seal tightly in plastic bags and refrigerate up to four

Herb Crepes

Makes twenty to twenty-two 6-inch crepes

1½ cups sifted all purpose flour
  1 cup milk
  1 cup water
  4 eggs
    Pinch of freshly grated nutmeg
    Pinch of salt
  ¼ cup (½ stick) unsalted butter, melted

1 tablespoon finely minced fresh parsley
1 tablespoon finely minced fresh chives

Butter

Combine first 4 ingredients with nutmeg and salt in processor or blender and mix until smooth, scraping sides of container as necessary. Pour into mixing bowl. Add melted butter and herbs and whisk until blended. Cover and let stand 2 hours at room temperature.

Heat 1 teaspoon butter in 6-inch crepe pan. Add just enough batter to coat bottom and brown crepe on each side. Repeat with remaining batter, adding more butter as necessary.

days, or overwrap with freezer paper and freeze several months. You might want to wrap and store them in more convenient groups of six or twelve depending on the quantity you will need at one time. Bring to room temperature before filling to avoid tearing.

After you have become a crepe-making expert, don't be afraid to be adventurous: Crepes can also be made with whole wheat flour or with coarser nonwheat flours such as buckwheat or chestnut. More liquid may be required for these. For a timesaving shortcut, use instant flour—the batter then needs only 30 minutes resting time before cooking. For extra-light crepes, replace some or all of the milk with water, beer, buttermilk, lowfat milk, meat stock or club soda. Use whipping cream or half and half instead of milk if richer crepes are desired.

Folding

There are ways to fold crepes other than the traditional roll-up method. Here are a few (remember always to spread filling over the second-cooked and less attractive side).

Jelly Roll: Spread layer of filling over crepe, leaving ½-inch border all around. Roll up tightly like a jelly roll. Arrange filled crepes seam side down in buttered baking dish.

Triangular Wedge: Spread layer of filling over crepe, leaving ½-inch border all around. Fold in half and then in half again to form triangle. Arrange in buttered baking dish, in overlapping pattern if desired (this is an especially nice presentation for dessert crepes).

Lapped Rectangle: Spoon generous amount of filling down center of crepe. Bring up two opposite sides and overlap on top of filling. Arrange seam side down in buttered baking dish.

Square Package: Spoon generous amount of filling down center of crepe. Bring up two opposite sides and overlap on top of filling. Bring up other two sides and overlap on top of crepe to form square package. Arrange seam side down in buttered baking dish.

Buckwheat Blini with Caviar and Smoked Salmon

Blini batter will keep several days in refrigerator. Allow 6 to 8 hours total preparation time if cooking blini batter the same day it is mixed. Be sure to cook blini over medium heat.

Makes about 3½ dozen 2-inch pancakes

2 cups warm milk (105°F to 115°F)
1 teaspoon dry yeast
½ teaspoon sugar
½ cup cake flour

2 egg yolks, room temperature
½ cup buckwheat flour
½ cup cake flour
¼ cup (½ stick) butter, melted and cooled
3 tablespoons sour cream, room temperature

¾ teaspoon salt
2 to 3 egg whites, room temperature
Pinch of salt
Pinch of cream of tartar

Butter
Melted clarified unsalted butter, fresh lemon juice, sour cream or crème fraîche, smoked salmon or gravlax and caviar (garnishes)

Combine ½ cup warm milk, yeast and sugar in small bowl and stir until yeast is dissolved. Let stand until foamy and proofed, about 10 minutes.

Pour ½ cup cake flour into large bowl and make well in center. Pour in yeast mixture with enough remaining warm milk to make thick paste. Mix gently until smooth (vigorous mixing will develop too much gluten). Stir in remaining milk. Cover with plastic wrap and let rise in warm draft-free area (85°F) until doubled, about 2 to 3 hours.

Add egg yolks, buckwheat flour and remaining ½ cup cake flour to batter and blend well. Cover and let rise in warm draft-free area until doubled, 2 to 3 hours. *(Batter can be prepared ahead to this point. When second rising is almost completed, cover and refrigerate overnight. Finish second rising next day.)*

Stir melted butter, sour cream and salt into batter. Combine egg whites, salt and cream of tartar in medium mixing bowl and beat until whites are stiff and glossy. Gently fold whites into batter. Cover and let rise in warm draft-free area for at least 30 minutes.

Melt butter on griddle or in heavy large skillet* over medium heat. Drop batter onto griddle by spoonfuls (do not crowd) and cook until bottom of blini is brown and top is filled with unbroken air bubbles. Turn and brown other side. Repeat with remaining batter, buttering griddle as necessary. Serve immediately or arrange in single layer on baking sheet and keep warm in low oven. Garnish as desired.

*For large blini, cook in 6-inch crepe pans or individual cast-iron skillets.

Quick Breads and Muffins

Pumpkin-Apple Bundt Bread

This bread freezes very well.

8 to 10 servings

2 cups unbleached all purpose flour (10 ounces)
1 tablespoon baking powder
½ teaspoon baking soda
½ teaspoon salt
½ teaspoon cinnamon
½ teaspoon freshly grated nutmeg
¼ teaspoon ground cloves
¼ teaspoon ground ginger
1½ cups sugar (10½ ounces)
2 eggs

½ cup plus 2 tablespoons (1¼ sticks) unsalted butter (room temperature), cut into 5 pieces
1 cup canned pumpkin puree
2 cups (about 2 large) loosely packed, unpeeled shredded tart apples (Granny Smith or greening)
2 tablespoons powdered sugar (optional)

Position rack in center of oven and preheat to 350°F. Generously butter 12-cup bundt pan; set aside.

If using food processor, mix first 8 ingredients; remove and set aside. Process sugar and eggs until fluffy. Add butter and process 1 minute. Add pumpkin puree and apples and process 2 seconds. Add dry ingredients, combining with as few on/off turns as possible to just blend flour into batter; *do not overprocess or texture will be coarse.*

If using mixer, combine first 8 ingredients and blend well; set aside. Cream butter and sugar in large mixing bowl. Add eggs and pumpkin and mix until fluffy. Add apples and blend thoroughly. Mix in dry ingredients.

Turn batter into prepared pan and bake until bread begins to pull away from sides of pan, about 50 to 55 minutes. Remove from oven and let stand on wire rack 5 minutes. Invert onto rack and cool completely. Press powdered sugar through sieve onto bread just before serving, if desired.

Scandinavian Apple Cake

This cake is great with coffee. Make it a week ahead, wrap in plastic and refrigerate. It will mellow and develop excellent flavor. Make several extra cakes to freeze; it will keep, frozen, for 3 months.

Makes 2 cakes, each 6 servings

4 large, tart apples, peeled, cored and chopped
1 cup sugar
1 cup chopped nuts
⅔ cup melted butter
2 eggs, beaten
2 teaspoons vanilla

2 cups sifted all purpose flour
2 teaspoons baking soda
2 teaspoons cinnamon
2 teaspoons allspice
1 teaspoon cardamom
½ teaspoon salt

Preheat oven to 350°F. Grease two 8- or 9-inch square cake pans.

Combine apples, sugar, nuts and butter in large bowl. Stir in eggs and vanilla. Sift together dry ingredients and add to apple mixture, stirring only until blended. Divide batter between pans and bake 45 to 50 minutes or until tester comes out clean. Cool on cake rack, wrap well and refrigerate. Serve at room temperature cut into bars.

Inverary Inn's Bonnach

A traditional, hearty Scottish bread, often served at breakfast.

Makes 1 loaf

3 cups all purpose flour
1 tablespoon baking powder
1 tablespoon sugar
1 teaspoon baking soda

1 teaspoon salt
1½ cups buttermilk
½ cup sour cream

Preheat oven to 350°F. Sift flour, baking powder, sugar, soda and salt into large mixing bowl. Repeat twice. Add buttermilk and sour cream and mix well. Form dough into ball and transfer to lightly floured surface (dough will be sticky). Roll dough into 12 × 7 × 1-inch oval; score top. Carefully transfer to ungreased baking sheet. Bake until loaf is golden brown, about 30 minutes. Cut into generous slices. Serve warm.

Best-Ever Banana Bread

Makes 1 loaf

2 ripe medium bananas, mashed
2 eggs
1¾ cups unsifted all purpose flour
1½ cups sugar
1 cup chopped walnuts

½ cup vegetable oil
¼ cup plus 1 tablespoon buttermilk
1 teaspoon baking soda
1 teaspoon vanilla
½ teaspoon salt

Preheat oven to 325°F. Grease and flour 9 × 5-inch loaf pan. Combine all ingredients in large bowl and mix well. Transfer to prepared pan. Bake until top is golden brown and splits slightly, about 1 hour and 20 minutes. Serve warm.

Do not double recipe.

Rhubarb Nut Bread

Makes two 9 × 5-inch loaves or four 5⅝ × 3⅛-inch loaves

1½ cups firmly packed brown sugar
¾ cup oil
1 egg
2½ cups unsifted all purpose flour
1 cup sour milk or 15 tablespoons milk mixed with 1 tablespoon white vinegar
1 teaspoon salt

1 teaspoon baking soda
1 teaspoon cinnamon
1 teaspoon vanilla
2½ cups chopped fresh or unsweetened frozen rhubarb*
½ cup chopped walnuts or pecans
½ cup sugar
1 tablespoon butter

Preheat oven to 325°F. Generously grease and flour loaf pans. Using electric mixer, beat brown sugar, oil and egg in large bowl. Add next 6 ingredients and mix on low speed. Fold in rhubarb and nuts. Turn into pans, spreading evenly. Thoroughly blend sugar and butter and sprinkle evenly over batter. Bake until bread pulls away from sides of pan, about 1 hour; *do not overbake*. Cool on wire rack before removing from pans. Wrap and store overnight to develop flavors.

*If rhubarb is frozen, do not thaw.

Mocha Yogurt Loaf

Makes 1 loaf

2 cups all purpose flour
2 tablespoons unsweetened cocoa powder
1 teaspoon baking powder
1 teaspoon baking soda
¼ teaspoon salt
2 egg whites, room temperature
¼ teaspoon cream of tartar
¼ cup sugar

¾ cup sugar
½ cup (1 stick) butter, room temperature
2 egg yolks
2 tablespoons instant coffee granules
⅔ cup plain yogurt
¼ cup strong coffee
⅔ cup finely chopped pecans

Preheat oven to 350°F. Generously grease 9 × 5-inch loaf pan. Line bottom and sides of pan with waxed paper.

Sift flour, cocoa, baking powder, baking soda and salt into medium bowl and set aside. Beat egg whites in large bowl of electric mixer at medium speed until foamy. Blend in cream of tartar. Gradually add ¼ cup sugar, beating until whites are stiff and glossy. Transfer to another bowl and set aside.

Combine ¾ cup sugar, butter, egg yolks and instant coffee granules in large bowl of electric mixer and beat at medium speed until light and fluffy. Reduce speed to low. Add flour mixture, yogurt and coffee alternately to egg mixture, beating after each addition just until blended. Stir in ⅓ of beaten egg whites. Fold in remaining whites; fold in pecans.

Transfer batter to prepared pan, smoothing top. Bake until tester inserted in center comes out clean, about 1 hour. Cool in pan on rack 10 minutes. Remove loaf from pan; discard waxed paper. Cool completely on rack before serving.

Sweet Corn Bread

Any leftover corn bread is delicious toasted and topped with honey.

4 to 6 servings

¼ cup (½ stick) butter
⅓ cup sugar
1 egg
1 cup water

1 cup cornmeal
1 cup all purpose flour
1¼ teaspoons baking powder
Pinch of salt

Preheat oven to 400°F. Grease 6 × 9-inch baking dish. Cream butter, sugar and egg in medium mixing bowl. Add water, cornmeal, flour, baking powder and salt. Pour into prepared baking dish. Bake until top is golden, about 20 to 25 minutes. Serve warm.

Fig Rum Loaf

Makes 1 loaf

1½ cups dried figs, cut into small
    pieces
1 cup sugar
3 tablespoons butter
½ teaspoon salt
1⅓ cups boiling water
2½ cups all purpose flour
1½ teaspoons baking soda

1 teaspoon baking powder
1 egg
3 tablespoons dark Jamaica rum
1 tablespoon freshly grated orange
    peel
¾ cup chopped walnuts

Preheat oven to 350°F. Generously grease 9 × 5-inch loaf pan. Line bottom and sides of pan with waxed paper.

Combine figs, sugar, butter and salt in large bowl of electric mixer. Add boiling water. Let cool to room temperature (butter does not have to melt). Sift flour, baking soda and baking powder into medium bowl.

Add flour mixture, egg, rum and orange peel to fig mixture and beat with electric mixer at medium speed until well blended. Stir in nuts. Transfer batter to prepared pan, smoothing top. Bake until tester inserted in center comes out clean, about 65 to 75 minutes. Let cool in pan on rack 10 minutes. Remove loaf from pan and discard waxed paper. Let cool completely on rack. Wrap airtight and let stand at least 24 hours before serving.

Almond Crumb Loaf

Makes 1 loaf

2 cups all purpose flour
1¼ cups sugar
2 teaspoons baking powder
¼ teaspoon salt
⅔ cup butter, room temperature
½ cup chopped sliced almonds

¾ teaspoon cinnamon
¼ teaspoon ground allspice
2 eggs
¾ cup milk
1 teaspoon vanilla extract
½ teaspoon almond extract

Preheat oven to 350°F. Generously grease 9 × 5-inch loaf pan. Line bottom and sides of pan with single piece of waxed paper, allowing 2-inch overhang of paper at top.

Sift flour, sugar, baking powder and salt into large bowl. Cut in butter until mixture resembles coarse meal. Transfer ½ cup of mixture to medium bowl. Add almonds, cinnamon and allspice and mix until well blended. Stir eggs, milk, vanilla and almond extracts into remaining mixture; beat until blended.

Pour about 1 cup batter into prepared pan. Sprinkle with ⅓ of nut mixture. Repeat twice, ending with nut mixture. Bake until tester inserted in center comes out clean, about 75 to 80 minutes. Let cool in pan on rack 15 minutes. Loosen sides of loaf from pan with wide spatula. Grasp waxed paper firmly and carefully pull loaf out of pan. Transfer to rack. Discard waxed paper. Let loaf cool on rack.

Blueberry Buckle

8 servings

2 cups sifted all purpose flour
2 teaspoons baking powder
½ teaspoon salt
¼ cup (½ stick) butter, room temperature
¾ cup sugar
1 egg
½ cup milk
2 cups fresh or thawed frozen unsweetened blueberries

Topping
½ cup sugar
⅓ cup sifted all purpose flour
¼ cup (½ stick) butter, room temperature
½ teaspoon cinnamon
Custard Sauce (see following recipe) or whipping cream

Preheat oven to 375°F. Generously butter 8 × 8-inch square baking pan. Sift together flour, baking powder and salt. Cream butter and sugar in medium bowl. Add egg and beat well. Gradually add flour mixture alternately with milk, beating well after each addition. Fold in berries. Pour evenly into pan.

Combine all ingredients for topping and blend well with fork. Distribute evenly over batter. Bake until lightly golden and toothpick inserted in center comes out clean, 35 to 40 minutes. Serve warm with Custard Sauce or cream.

Custard Sauce

Makes about 2 cups

3 tablespoons sugar
½ teaspoon cornstarch
3 egg yolks

2 cups milk
½ teaspoon lemon extract
Pinch of salt

Combine sugar and cornstarch in small dish and blend well. Beat yolks in small bowl. Gradually add sugar mixture. Scald milk in top of double boiler over hot water. Gradually blend in egg mixture. Continue cooking, stirring constantly, until custard coats spoon, about 5 to 6 minutes. Cool completely, stirring occasionally. Add lemon extract and salt. Serve at room temperature.

Brown Rice Raisin Muffins

Makes 12 to 16 muffins

⅔ cup unbleached flour
½ cup whole wheat flour
1 tablespoon baking powder
1 teaspoon salt
⅔ cup milk

¼ cup oil
2 eggs, lightly beaten
2 tablespoons honey
½ cup cooked brown rice
½ cup raisins

Preheat oven to 375°F. Lightly grease 12 regular or 16 small muffin cups.

Mix dry ingredients together in large bowl. In separate bowl, combine milk, oil, eggs and honey and blend well. Stir into dry ingredients only enough to moisten. Blend in rice and raisins. Spoon into muffin cups and bake 20 to 25 minutes or until lightly browned.

Bran Muffins

Makes 2 dozen

2 cups all purpose flour
1½ cups natural bran
1½ teaspoons baking soda
½ teaspoon salt

2 cups plain yogurt
¾ cup raisins
½ cup oil
½ cup dark molasses

Preheat oven to 425°F. Generously grease muffin tins. Thoroughly combine dry ingredients in large mixing bowl. Make well in center and add remaining ingredients, blending just until moist; do not overmix. Divide among tins. Bake until muffins test done, about 25 minutes.

Walnut Corn Bran Muffins

Makes about 1 dozen muffins

1 cup milk
½ cup bran flakes

Walnut oil
¼ cup (½ stick) unsalted butter
3 tablespoons dark brown sugar
1 egg, room temperature
1 teaspoon walnut oil (optional)

1 cup all purpose flour
½ cup cornmeal
½ cup toasted walnuts, coarsely chopped
2 teaspoons baking powder
½ teaspoon salt

Combine milk and bran flakes in medium bowl and let stand at room temperature for 8 hours or overnight.

Preheat oven to 400°F. Generously coat twelve 2½-inch muffin cups with walnut oil. Cream ¼ cup butter with sugar in large mixing bowl. Stir in egg and walnut oil, blending well. Fold in flour, cornmeal, walnuts, baking powder, salt and bran mixture until dry ingredients are just moistened. Divide batter evenly among muffin cups. Bake until muffins are brown and tester inserted in centers comes out clean, 20 to 25 minutes. Cool in pan about 7 minutes and serve.

Yeast Breads and Cakes

Spiced Dark Bread with Currants

Moist, chewy and fragrant, this bread is reminiscent of an old-fashioned raisin pumpernickel loaf.

Makes 1 loaf

1¼ cups water
5 tablespoons unsulphured molasses
2 tablespoons (¼ stick) unsalted butter
1 ounce unsweetened chocolate, chopped
2 teaspoons dry yeast

2 cups medium or dark rye flour (7½ ounces)
1 cup Yogurt Bread Starter (see

following recipe), warmed to room temperature over bowl of lukewarm water (80°F to 90°F)
½ cup rolled oats
1½ teaspoons ground ginger
1½ teaspoons salt
1 teaspoon ground cloves
1 teaspoon cinnamon
2 to 3 cups bread flour (10 to 15 ounces)

⅔ cup currants

Grease large bowl and set aside. Combine water, molasses, butter and chocolate in small saucepan over medium-low heat and warm slowly to 100°F. Blend in yeast. Remove mixture from heat and let stand until bubbly and proofed, about 10 to 12 minutes.

Combine rye flour, starter, oats, ginger, salt, cloves, cinnamon and molasses mixture in processor and mix 10 seconds, or until batter is sticky and elastic. Transfer to mixing bowl. Beat in enough bread flour to form stiff, slightly sticky dough. Knead until slightly elastic, about 15 minutes. Transfer dough to prepared bowl, turning to coat all surfaces. Cover with plastic and let stand at room temperature until doubled, about 3 hours.

Generously grease 8-inch springform pan. Punch dough down. Cover and let rise again until doubled in volume, about 2 more hours.

Lightly flour currants, shaking off excess. Stir into dough. Turn dough out onto lightly floured surface and flatten with palms of hands. Shape dough into ball. Arrange in prepared pan and flatten slightly. Cover with towel and let rise again until doubled in volume, about 3 more hours.

Position rack in lower third of oven and preheat to 450°F. Place bread in oven and immediately reduce temperature to 375°F. Bake 40 minutes. Reduce temperature to 325°F and continue baking until bottom of loaf sounds hollow when tapped, about 10 to 15 minutes. Turn out onto rack to cool before slicing and serving.

Yogurt Bread Starter

Store starter in the refrigerator, stirring once a week. Each time it is used, replenish it with ½ cup warm water (90°F) and ½ cup rye or whole wheat flour, then cover and allow to stand in a warm draft-free area until mixture is bubbly. Store covered in the refrigerator for several days to reactivate. Starter requires 4 days initial preparation.

Makes 2 quarts

2 cups light or medium rye flour (7 ounces)
1 cup plain yogurt, room temperature
¾ cup warm water (90°F)
2½ tablespoons cider vinegar
1 tablespoon dry yeast
½ teaspoon crushed caraway seed
½ teaspoon ground cardamom

To be added each of last three days:
1 cup light or medium rye flour (3½ ounces)
2 tablespoons brown sugar dissolved in ¾ cup warm water (90°F)

Combine 2 cups rye flour with yogurt, water, vinegar, yeast, caraway and cardamom in large bowl and beat until well blended. Cover and let stand at warm room temperature for 24 hours.

Beat in 1 cup rye flour with brown sugar mixture. Let stand at warm room temperature another 24 hours.

Repeat procedure with same amount of flour, brown sugar and warm water. Let stand another 24 hours.

Repeat procedure with same amount of flour, sugar and warm water. Let stand 12 to 24 hours. *(Can be used immediately or refrigerated until needed.)*

Walnut Wheat Bread

Makes 2 loaves

¼ cup warm water (105°F to 115°F)
1 envelope dry yeast
1 cup milk

3 cups whole wheat flour (or more)
2 tablespoons (¼ stick) butter, room temperature

1 tablespoon sugar
1 teaspoon salt

1 cup walnut halves
Softened butter

Melted butter

Generously butter large mixing bowl and two 7 × 3-inch loaf pans. Combine water and yeast in small bowl and let stand until foamy and proofed, about 10 minutes. Meanwhile, pour 1 cup milk into small saucepan. Place over medium-high heat and scald. Let cool to lukewarm. Stir into yeast mixture.

Combine 3 cups flour with butter, sugar and salt in processor and mix using on/off turns just until blended. With machine running, add yeast mixture through feed tube in slow steady stream and mix 60 seconds, adding more flour if necessary (dough should be slightly sticky at this point).

Turn dough out onto floured surface and knead until smooth and elastic, about 1 to 2 minutes. Form into ball. Transfer to prepared bowl, turning to coat entire surface. Cover with plastic wrap and let rise in warm draft-free area (85°F) until doubled in volume, approximately 1¼ hours.

Punch dough down and knead several times. Let rest 10 minutes. Turn dough out onto floured surface and divide in half. Roll each half into 12 × 6-inch rectangle. Gently push about 13 walnut halves into each. Roll up rectangles, folding ends under. Rub top and sides of loaves with softened butter. Transfer to prepared pans. Let stand in warm draft-free area until doubled, 1 hour.

Preheat oven to 375°F. Center walnut half on each loaf for decoration. Brush tops with melted butter. Bake until loaves sound hollow when tapped on bottom, about 35 minutes. Transfer to rack to cool. Slice thinly to serve.

Jane's Sweet Whole Wheat Bread

8 servings

1 envelope dry yeast
¼ cup warm water (105°F to 115°F)

1 cup milk, scalded and cooled to lukewarm
2 cups whole wheat flour

½ cup packed light brown sugar
⅓ cup yellow cornmeal
2 teaspoons salt
1 cup all purpose flour

Lightly grease mixing bowl and set aside. Sprinkle yeast over warm water in small bowl and let stand until foamy and proofed, about 10 minutes.

Pour lukewarm milk into large bowl. Blend in yeast mixture. Stir in whole wheat flour, brown sugar, cornmeal and salt with wooden spoon (or use dough hook of electric mixer) until completely blended. Transfer dough to lightly floured surface and knead, gradually adding all purpose flour, until dough has absorbed as much flour as possible without becoming stiff. Knead dough until smooth, about 15 minutes.

Gather dough into ball. Transfer to prepared bowl, turning to coat entire surface. Cover with damp towel and let rise in warm draft-free area until doubled, about 2½ to 3 hours.

Generously butter 2 baking sheets. Punch dough down. Divide in half and shape into round loaves. Transfer to prepared baking sheets. Let rise in warm draft-free area until doubled in volume, about 1½ hours.

Preheat oven to 350°F. Bake bread until browned (covering with foil if it begins browning too fast) and loaves sound hollow when tapped, about 40 minutes. Cool on rack before slicing.

Sourdough English Muffins

Makes 1 dozen muffins

1 package dry yeast
½ cup lukewarm water (90°F to 105°F)
½ cup Basic Sourdough Starter (see recipe, page 50), room temperature
⅓ cup instant nonfat dry milk

2½ teaspoons sugar
¾ teaspoon salt
¾ cup lukewarm water (90°F to 105°F)
3 to 3¾ cups all purpose flour

Cornmeal

Grease large bowl and set aside. Dissolve yeast in ½ cup lukewarm water in another large bowl and let stand 5 minutes to proof. Add starter, dry milk, sugar and salt and blend well. Mix in remaining water. Add 3 cups flour and beat until smooth. Turn dough out onto lightly floured surface and knead until smooth and elastic, adding remaining ¾ cup flour as necessary. Transfer dough to greased bowl, turning to coat all surfaces. Cover with plastic and let stand in warm draft-free area until doubled, 1 to 1½ hours.

Sprinkle work surface and baking sheet with cornmeal. Punch dough down and turn out onto surface. Roll to thickness of about ½ inch. Cut into rounds using 3-inch cutter. Place rounds cornmeal side up on baking sheet. Cover and let stand in warm draft-free area until almost doubled, about 1 hour.

Preheat griddle to 275°F; grease lightly. Cook muffins on both sides until lightly browned, turning once, about 10 minutes per side. Transfer to wire rack and let cool. Store in airtight plastic bags. Split and toast just before serving.

Basic Croissants

Makes 24 croissants

2 envelopes dry yeast
¾ cup warm water (105°F to 115°F)
3¾ cups unbleached all purpose flour
½ cup milk
2 tablespoons sugar
2 teaspoons salt

2 cups (4 sticks) unsalted butter, well chilled and cut into ½-inch pieces

1 egg beaten with 1 tablespoon milk

Combine yeast and water in medium bowl and stir until yeast dissolves. Add ¾ cup flour with milk and sugar and whisk until smooth. Cover bowl with plastic wrap. Let stand in warm area, about 75°F, 1½ to 2 hours to mature. (An oven preheated to lowest setting 1 minute and then turned off works well.) About halfway through rising process, batter will bubble up, then sink down; if preparation is to be discontinued at this point, stir bubbles out of batter and refrigerate up to 24 hours; maturing process will continue.

Combine remaining 3 cups flour with salt in large bowl. Add well-chilled butter and mix, flattening butter pieces slightly between fingertips and working quickly so butter remains firm. (Refrigerate mixture if yeast batter is not ready to use.) Pour yeast batter into flour mixture and fold in using large rubber spatula, just moistening flour without breaking up butter pieces; dough will be crumbly.

To fold dough: Turn dough out onto lightly floured surface. Pat dough down and roll into 18 × 12-inch rectangle; if dough is sticky, sprinkle top lightly with flour. Using metal spatula or pastry sheet, fold right ⅓ of dough toward center, then fold left ⅓ over to cover (as for business letter); dough will still be slightly rough. Lift folded dough off work surface, scrape surface clean and sprinkle lightly with flour. Repeat patting, rolling and folding dough 3 more times. *(If butter starts to soften and run, immediately wrap dough in plastic and freeze 10 to 15 minutes; butter pieces must remain layered throughout dough to ensure flaky pastry.)* Wrap in plastic and chill at least 45 minutes (or up to 24 hours).

To shape croissants: Pat dough into rough rectangle. Cut in half lengthwise through center, then crosswise into thirds, forming 6 equal pieces. Return 5 pieces to refrigerator. Roll remaining piece out on well-floured surface into 5½ × 14-inch rectangle. Using pastry cutter or long sharp knife, divide dough in half crosswise to form two 5½ × 7-inch pieces. Cut each piece diagonally to form a total of 4 triangles. Using rolling pin, gently roll across shortest side of 1 triangle, until dough measures 7 inches across. Gently roll from longest side to point until dough measures 8 inches across. Holding point of triangle with one hand, loosely roll dough up from base to point with the other hand. Transfer croissants tip side down to ungreased rimmed baking sheet. Curve both ends down slightly, forming crescent. Repeat with remaining dough.

Brush croissants with egg mixture. Set aside, uncovered, in warm area (70°F to 75°F) and let rise until doubled in volume, about 1 to 2 hours; reglaze with egg mixture once during rising.

To bake: Position rack in center of oven and preheat to 450°F. Reglaze croissants with egg mixture. Bake until puffed and golden brown, about 12 to 15 minutes. Let cool on rack at least 10 minutes before serving. *(Croissants can be cooled completely, wrapped airtight and frozen. Reheat unthawed croissants in 375°F oven for 10 minutes.)*

Petits Pains au Chocolat

Your favorite chocolate bar—with or without nuts—can be used here.

Makes 32 pastries

1 recipe Basic Croissant dough, ready for shaping (see page 70)
6 ounces semisweet or milk chocolate, coarsely chopped
1 egg beaten with 1 tablespoon milk

Divide croissant dough into 4 equal pieces. Return 3 pieces to refrigerator. Roll remaining piece out on lightly floured surface into rectangle slightly larger than 10 × 12 inches. Using pastry wheel, trim dough to exactly 10 × 12-inch rectangle. Divide into eight 6 × 2½-inch rectangles. Sprinkle 2 teaspoons chocolate across each rectangle, leaving 1-inch border at each end. Starting at 1 short end, roll dough up around chocolate; do not seal ends of roll. Arrange rolls seam side down on ungreased rimmed baking sheet. Brush rolls with egg mixture. Repeat with remaining croissant dough.

Set dough aside, uncovered, in warm area (70°F to 75°F) and let rise until almost doubled in volume, about 1½ hours; reglaze once during rising.

Position rack in center of oven and preheat to 450°F. Brush rolls with egg mixture. Cut several ⅛ inch deep diagonal lines across top for decoration. Bake until golden, 15 to 20 minutes. Cool on racks and serve at room temperature.

Whole Wheat Croissants

Makes 24 croissants

2 envelopes dry yeast
¾ cup warm water (105°F to 115°F)
1¾ cups whole wheat flour
½ cup milk
1½ tablespoons honey

1¾ cups unbleached all purpose flour

2 teaspoons salt
2 cups (4 sticks) unsalted butter, well chilled and cut into ½-inch pieces

1 egg beaten with 1 tablespoon milk

Combine yeast and water in medium bowl and stir until yeast dissolves. Add ¾ cup whole wheat flour with milk and honey and whisk until smooth. Cover bowl with plastic wrap. Let stand in warm area, about 75°F, 1½ to 2 hours to mature. (An oven preheated to lowest setting 1 minute and then turned off works well.) About halfway through rising process, batter will bubble up, then sink down; if preparation is to be discontinued at this point, stir bubbles out of batter and refrigerate up to 24 hours; maturing process will continue in refrigerator.

Combine remaining 1 cup whole wheat flour with 1¾ cups all purpose flour and 2 teaspoons salt in large bowl. Add well-chilled butter and mix, flattening butter pieces slightly between fingertips and working quickly so that butter remains firm. (Refrigerate mixture if yeast batter is not ready to use.) Pour yeast batter into flour mixture and carefully fold in using rubber spatula, just moistening flour without breaking up butter pieces; dough will be rough and crumbly.

Fold, shape, glaze and bake dough following directions for Basic Croissants (see recipe, page 70).

Cheese Croissants

Makes 24 croissants

1 recipe Basic or Whole Wheat Croissant dough (see pages 70–71), ready for rolling
1½ cups freshly grated cheese (Gruyère, Swiss, Emmenthal, cheddar, Parmesan or mix)
1 egg beaten with 1 tablespoon milk

Roll dough out into 12 × 18-inch rectangle. Sprinkle ¼ of cheese crosswise on middle third of dough. Fold right ⅓ of dough over cheese. Sprinkle another ¼ of cheese on top of flap. Fold left ⅓ of dough over to cover (as for business letter). Roll out again into 12 × 18-inch rectangle. Repeat folding, using remaining cheese. Wrap dough in plastic and refrigerate at least 30 minutes (or up to 24 hours).

Shape, glaze and bake dough following directions for Basic Croissants (see recipe, page 70).

Fruit and Marzipan Brioche

Brioche can be made ahead and frozen. Reheat without thawing in a 300°F oven for about 20 to 25 minutes.

Makes 2 brioches

¼ cup warm water (105°F to 115°F)
1 envelope dry yeast
1 teaspoon sugar

½ cup warm milk (105°F to 115°F)
2 to 3½ cups all purpose flour
¼ cup sugar
1 teaspoon salt
3 eggs (room temperature)
½ cup (1 stick) unsalted butter, cut into 8 pieces (room temperature)

Filling
¾ pound almond paste
¾ cup ground almonds

½ cup light raisins
½ cup finely chopped glacéed cherries and pineapple or mixed glacéed fruit
2 egg whites
¼ teaspoon almond extract

1 egg
2 to 3 tablespoons milk
Sliced almonds (decoration)

Powdered sugar (optional)

Combine water, yeast and 1 teaspoon sugar in large mixing bowl and stir until yeast is dissolved. Let stand until foamy and proofed, about 5 minutes.

Add milk, 3 cups flour, sugar, salt and eggs and blend lightly. Add butter and mix until soft dough is formed (use hands or wooden spoon).

Pick up dough and slap back into bowl to knead, adding flour as necessary until dough is smooth and no longer sticky (this will take about 100 slaps, or 10 to 15 minutes). Gather dough into ball and place in lightly greased bowl, turning to coat entire surface. Cover and let rise in warm area (85°F) until doubled in volume, 1 to 2 hours.

For filling: Combine almond paste, almonds, raisins, fruit, egg whites and extract and mix well. Divide in half. Form each half into roughly shaped rectangle and place between 2 sheets of waxed paper. Roll into 8-inch squares. Refrigerate 45 to 60 minutes so mixture will be easier to work with.

Punch dough down. Turn out onto lightly *oiled* surface and knead a few minutes. Cut off ⅕ of dough and set aside; divide remaining dough in half; roll each piece into 10-inch square.

Peel top sheet of waxed paper from half of filling. Place filling side down onto 1 square of dough and peel off remaining paper. Roll dough jelly roll fashion, stretching to make strand 14 to 15 inches long. Bring ends together to form ring. Place seam side down in buttered 1-quart brioche pan. Repeat with remaining filling and dough square.

Divide reserved dough in half; form each half into teardrop shape and insert point into center of dough rings. Cover and let rise in warm area until almost doubled, about 45 to 60 minutes.

Place rack in lower third of oven and preheat to 350°F. Combine egg and milk and brush over top of brioche. Sprinkle with sliced almonds. Bake until skewer inserted into center comes out clean, 40 to 45 minutes.

Let stand 10 minutes, then remove from pans and let cool slightly. Dust with powdered sugar, if desired. Cut into wedges and serve warm.

Savarin with Blueberries

8 large servings or 10 to 12 small servings

Dough
- 2 cups all purpose flour
- 6 tablespoons warm milk (105°F to 115°F)
- 2 tablespoons sugar
- 1 envelope dry yeast
  Pinch of salt

- 6 tablespoons (¾ stick) butter, room temperature
- 4 eggs
- 2 tablespoons raisins, plumped in water, drained

Syrup (see following recipe)

Apricot Glaze
- 1 11-ounce jar apricot preserves
- ¼ cup water
  Grated zest of 1 lemon
- 2 tablespoons Cointreau

- 2 cups blueberries
  Crème fraîche

Generously butter 8-cup ring mold and large mixing bowl; set aside.

Combine ½ cup flour, milk, sugar, yeast and salt in small mixing bowl and beat with wooden spoon until smooth. Let stand until frothy, about 25 minutes.

Combine remaining flour, butter and eggs in another mixing bowl and blend well. Add yeast mixture and beat until dough is smooth and elastic, 3 to 4 minutes. Add raisins and blend well. Turn into prepared bowl, cover and let rise in warm area until doubled, 45 to 60 minutes.

Punch dough down and transfer to prepared mold, filling evenly. Cover and let rise in warm place until it reaches top of mold, about 45 minutes.

About 15 minutes before ready to bake, preheat oven to 375°F. Bake until savarin is golden and knife inserted in center comes out clean, about 20 minutes.

While savarin is baking, prepare syrup. When savarin is done, unmold onto serving platter and, using sharp-pronged fork, make holes over entire surface of cake. Spoon syrup over warm savarin, basting every 10 to 15 minutes until all syrup is absorbed. Set aside.

For glaze: Combine preserves, water and zest in small heavy-bottomed saucepan over medium heat and cook, stirring occasionally, until preserves are melted. Remove from heat and stir in liqueur. Strain sauce through fine sieve. Spread evenly over savarin. Fill center with blueberries and pass crème fraîche.

Syrup

- 3 cups water
- 2¼ cups sugar

- ½ cup Cointreau
- 2 to 3 tablespoons Cognac

Combine water and sugar in heavy-bottomed medium saucepan. Bring to boil over high heat, stirring until sugar dissolves, then boil 3 minutes. Remove from heat and add liqueur and Cognac.

Sourdough Sour Cream Coffee Cake

8 to 10 servings

Streusel
½ cup chopped nuts
⅓ cup firmly packed brown sugar
¼ cup sugar
2 tablespoons (¼ stick) butter, cut into small pieces
1 teaspoon cinnamon

Cake
½ cup (1 stick) butter, room temperature
1 cup sugar

½ cup Basic Sourdough Starter (see recipe, page 50), room temperature
2 eggs
1 teaspoon vanilla
2 cups all purpose flour
1 teaspoon baking soda
1 teaspoon baking powder
½ teaspoon salt
1 cup sour cream
Powdered sugar

For streusel: Combine all ingredients in small bowl and set aside.

Preheat oven to 350°F. Grease 9- or 10-inch bundt pan. Cream butter with sugar in large bowl. Add starter, eggs and vanilla and beat until smooth. Sift dry ingredients and add alternately to creamed mixture with sour cream, beating well after each addition. Pour half of batter into pan and sprinkle with half of streusel mixture. Cover with remaining batter and top with remaining streusel. Bake until tester inserted in center of cake comes out clean, about 45 minutes. Remove cake from pan and let cool on wire rack. Sprinkle with powdered sugar before serving.

Alsatian Kugelhupf

A very simple batter bread, with a fresh lemon flavor. Kugelhupf is popular as a Christmas bread in Austria and Germany as well as Alsace.

Makes about 12 servings

¼ cup warm water (105°F to 115°F)
1 envelope dry yeast
¾ cup warm milk (105°F to 115°F)

¾ cup (1½ sticks) unsalted butter or margarine (room temperature)
½ cup sugar
4 eggs (room temperature)
4 cups all purpose flour
1 teaspoon salt

1 cup light raisins
½ cup slivered almonds
1 tablespoon finely grated lemon peel

Whole almonds
½ cup finely minced almonds

Powdered sugar (garnish)

Combine water and yeast in small bowl and stir until yeast is dissolved. Add milk and let stand until foamy and proofed, about 5 minutes.

Cream butter and sugar in large bowl of electric mixer. Add eggs and beat until fluffy. Blend in dissolved yeast. Sift in flour and salt and beat at low or medium speed until smooth. Stir in raisins, slivered almonds and lemon peel.

Butter 2-quart mold (preferably Kugelhupf, "turk's head," bundt or other attractive shape). Place whole almonds into design points and sprinkle mold with minced almonds.

For an airy but more coarsely textured bread, turn batter immediately into mold and let rise, then bake. For a closer textured, finer crumbed bread, let dough rise once in bowl until doubled, about 2 hours, then beat batter down, turn into mold and let rise again until within ¼ inch of top of mold.

Preheat oven to 375°F (for tube pan) or to 350°F for other pans. Bake until wooden skewer inserted into center of bread comes out clean, about 50 to 60 minutes if oven is at higher temperature, or 65 to 70 minutes at lower temperature. Let bread cool in pan 5 minutes. Turn onto serving board or plate and dust with powdered sugar. Slice into wedges and serve hot.

Yeast Ring with Streusel Topping

2 servings

Yeast Ring
1 cup warm milk (105°F to 115°F)
2 envelopes dry yeast
2 teaspoons sugar

3 cups unbleached all purpose flour (15 ounces)
⅓ cup sugar
½ teaspoon salt
3 egg yolks
1 teaspoon vanilla
¾ cup (1½ sticks) unsalted butter (room temperature), cut into 9 pieces

Streusel Topping
½ cup sugar (3½ ounces)
⅓ cup unbleached all purpose flour
¼ cup (½ stick) chilled unsalted butter, cut into 4 pieces
¼ teaspoon cinnamon
Pinch of salt

Filling
¾ cup golden raisins
¼ cup sugar
½ teaspoon cinnamon

For yeast ring: Combine milk, yeast and sugar and let proof until foam rises to surface, about 10 minutes.

Using mixer fitted with dough hook, or wooden spoon, combine flour, sugar and salt and blend well. Add yeast, yolks and vanilla and mix thoroughly. Add butter and beat until blended. *Dough should be thoroughly mixed and does not require kneading.* Cover tightly and chill 4 hours or overnight.

For streusel topping: Combine all ingredients using pastry blender, or processor with on/off turns, until mixture resembles coarse meal. Cover and chill.

Generously butter angel food cake pan with removable center or, for one-piece pan, line bottom with buttered waxed paper and generously butter sides and tube. Turn dough out onto well-floured board and divide in half. Roll each half into 7 × 13-inch rectangle.

Working quickly, sprinkle raisins evenly over dough and press into place with rolling pin. Sprinkle evenly with sugar and cinnamon. Roll each half up lengthwise, jelly roll fashion, then roll gently with hands so each half is 14 inches long. Place one "jelly roll" seam side down around center tube, bringing ends together. Top with second "jelly roll" seam side down so tucked ends rest on top of thickest part of first ring. (Do not have ends of both rings on top of each other or bread will not rise evenly.) Cover with damp towel and let stand in warm draft-free area until almost doubled, about 1¼ to 1¾ hours.

Fifteen minutes before baking, position rack in center of oven and preheat to 350°F. Sprinkle streusel crumbs lightly over top of dough. Bake 55 to 60 minutes. Remove from oven and let stand in pan on wire rack 10 minutes. Remove outer rim of pan and cool 30 minutes. Remove carefully from center stem and cool completely.

 *Pastries*

Kathleen McLean's Apricot Pastry

Makes 16 pastries

Apricot Filling
40 moist-pack pitted apricot halves
¼ cup sugar
1 teaspoon fresh lemon juice
¼ teaspoon almond extract

1 recipe Basic Whole Wheat Danish Pastry Dough (see following recipe)

⅓ cup chopped toasted pecans
1 egg beaten with 1 tablespoon milk

½ cup apricot preserves
2 tablespoons apricot brandy

For filling: Combine apricot halves with enough boiling water to cover in small bowl. Cover with plate or lid and let stand for several hours or overnight. Drain well. Transfer to food processor or blender and mix until pureed. Add sugar, lemon juice and almond extract and blend mixture well.

Line 2 rimmed baking sheets with parchment paper. Divide dough into 4 pieces. Return 3 pieces to refrigerator. Roll remaining piece out on lightly floured surface to form rectangle slightly larger than 9 × 12 inches. Using ruler and pastry wheel, trim dough to rectangle exactly 9 × 12 inches. Divide into four 4½ × 6-inch pieces. Spread 1 heaping tablespoon apricot filling in about 1-inch strip down center of dough. Sprinkle with 1 teaspoon pecans. Cut ½-inch-wide slits from edge of filling to edge of dough on both sides, slanting downward slightly (about 30 degree angle). Cut off triangular pieces at top of series of slits. Starting at top, fold 1 strip over filling. Fold opposite strip over. Repeat, forming mock braid. Press last 2 strips down to seal. Cut off excess dough at end. Transfer pastries to prepared baking sheet. Brush with egg mixture. Repeat with remaining dough. Let dough rest at room temperature for 30 minutes (dough will rise only slightly).

Position rack in center of oven and preheat to 450°F. Reglaze pastries with egg mixture. Transfer pastries to oven and reduce temperature to 400°F. Bake until golden, about 15 minutes.

Meanwhile, heat preserves in small saucepan. Press through sieve. Return puree to pan and reheat. Stir in apricot brandy. Brush warm glaze over pastries. Let cool slightly on wire rack. Serve warm or at room temperature.

Basic Whole Wheat Danish Pastry Dough

Makes 1 recipe

2 eggs, room temperature
   Warm water (105°F to 115°F)
2 envelopes dry yeast
1¾ cups whole wheat flour
½ cup milk, warmed to 115°F
3 tablespoons honey
1 teaspoon vanilla

2 cups all purpose flour

2 teaspoons salt
2 cups (4 sticks) unsalted butter, well chilled and cut into ½-inch pieces

Combine eggs in 1-cup measure with enough warm water to equal ¾ cup total. Transfer to medium bowl. Stir in yeast. Let stand until mixture bubbles, about 5 minutes. Whisk in ¾ cup whole wheat flour with milk, honey and vanilla and stir until smooth. Cover bowl with plastic wrap. Place in warm area (about 75°F) 1½ to 2 hours to mature (oven preheated to lowest setting 1 minute and then turned off works well). About halfway into rising process, batter will bubble up, then sink down; if preparation is to be discontinued at this point, stir bubbles out of batter and refrigerate up to 24 hours; maturing will continue in refrigerator.

Combine remaining 1 cup whole wheat flour with all purpose flour and salt in large bowl. Add well-chilled butter and mix, flattening butter pieces slightly between fingertips and working quickly so butter remains firm. (To ensure flaky layers, butter should remain in pieces the size of lima beans and should not be totally incorporated into dough.) Refrigerate mixture if yeast batter is not ready to use. Pour yeast batter into flour mixture and carefully fold in using large rubber spatula, just moistening flour mixture without breaking up any of butter pieces; dough will be crumbly.

Turn dough out onto surface lightly floured with all purpose flour. Pat dough down and roll into 12 × 18-inch rectangle; if dough is sticky, sprinkle top lightly with flour, brushing off excess. Using metal spatula, fold right ⅓ of dough toward center, then fold left ⅓ over to cover (as for business letter); dough will still be slightly rough. Lift folded dough from work surface, scrape surface clean and sprinkle lightly with flour. Repeat patting, rolling and folding 3 more times. *(If butter starts to soften and run, wrap dough in plastic and freeze 10 to 15 minutes; butter pieces must remain layered throughout dough to ensure flakiness.)* Cover with plastic wrap and chill at least 45 minutes (or up to 24 hours).

Almond Combs

Makes 3 dozen

Nut Filling
- 1 cup ground toasted almonds*
- ¼ cup (½ stick) butter, room temperature
- 3 tablespoons sugar
- 1½ tablespoons dark rum (optional)
- 1 egg, beaten
- ¼ teaspoon almond extract
- ¼ teaspoon vanilla extract

- 1 recipe Basic Danish Pastry Dough (see following recipe)
- 1 egg beaten with 1 tablespoon milk

- ¼ cup apricot preserves
- Sliced toasted almonds (garnish)

For filling: Combine ground almonds, butter, sugar, rum, egg, almond and vanilla extracts in medium bowl.

Line 2 rimmed baking sheets with parchment paper. Divide dough into 4 pieces. Return 3 pieces to refrigerator. Roll remaining piece out on lightly floured surface to form square slightly larger than 12 × 12 inches. Using ruler and pastry wheel, trim dough to square exactly 12 × 12 inches. Divide into nine 4-inch squares. Spread 2 teaspoons filling in ¾-inch-thick strip in center of right half of each square. Brush egg mixture around filling. Fold left side over filling, pressing to seal edges. Using very sharp knife, make eight to ten 1-inch-long perpendicular slashes along folded side of pastry. Spread pastry slightly at slashes. Transfer to prepared baking sheet. Repeat with remaining dough. Brush pastries with egg mixture. Let rest at room temperature 30 minutes (dough will rise only slightly). Reglaze with egg mixture.

Position rack in center of oven and preheat to 450°F. Transfer pastries to oven and immediately reduce temperature to 400°F. Bake until golden brown, about 12 to 15 minutes.

Meanwhile, press apricot preserves through fine strainer into small saucepan and bring to boil over medium heat. Remove from heat. Remove pastries from oven and transfer to wire rack. Immediately brush with apricot glaze. Press almonds into tops. Serve warm or at room temperature.

*Hazelnuts can be substituted for almonds.

Basic Danish Pastry Dough

Makes 1 recipe

2 **eggs, room temperature**
  Warm water (105°F to 115°F)
2 **envelopes dry yeast**
3¾ **cups unbleached all purpose flour**
½ **cup milk, warmed to 115°F**
¼ **cup sugar**

1 **teaspoon vanilla**
2 **teaspoons salt**
2 **cups (4 sticks) unsalted butter, well chilled and cut into ½-inch pieces**

Combine eggs in 1-cup measure with enough warm water to equal ¾ cup total. Transfer to medium bowl. Stir in yeast. Let stand until mixture bubbles, about 5 minutes. Whisk in ¾ cup flour with milk, sugar and vanilla and stir until smooth. Cover bowl with plastic wrap. Let stand in warm area (about 75°F) 1½ to 2 hours to mature (an oven preheated to lowest setting 1 minute and then turned off works well). About halfway through rising process, batter will bubble up, then sink down; if preparation is to be discontinued at this point, stir bubbles out of batter and refrigerate up to 24 hours; maturing process will continue.

Combine remaining 3 cups flour with salt in large bowl. Add well-chilled butter and mix, flattening butter pieces slightly between fingertips and working quickly so butter remains firm. (To ensure flaky layers, butter should remain in pieces the size of lima beans and should not be totally incorporated into dough.) Refrigerate mixture if yeast batter is not ready to use. Pour yeast batter into flour mixture and carefully fold in using large rubber spatula, just moistening flour mixture without breaking up any of butter pieces; dough will be crumbly.

Turn dough out onto lightly floured surface. Pat dough down and roll into 12 × 18-inch rectangle; if dough is sticky, sprinkle top lightly with flour, brushing off excess. Using metal spatula, fold right ⅓ of dough toward center, then fold left ⅓ over to cover (as for business letter); dough will still be slightly rough. Lift folded dough from work surface, scrape surface clean and sprinkle lightly with flour. Repeat patting, rolling and folding dough 3 more times. (*If butter starts to soften and run, immediately wrap dough in plastic and freeze 10 to 15 minutes; butter pieces must remain layered throughout dough to ensure flaky pastry.*) Cover dough with plastic wrap and refrigerate for at least 45 minutes (or up to 24 hours).

Strawberry Pinwheels

Makes 32 pinwheels

1 **recipe Basic Danish Pastry Dough (see recipe, above)**
⅔ **cup strawberry jam**
1 **egg beaten with 1 tablespoon milk**

1 **cup powdered sugar**

Line 2 rimmed baking sheets with parchment paper. Divide dough into 4 pieces. Return 3 pieces to refrigerator. Roll remaining piece out on lightly floured surface to form rectangle slightly larger than 8 × 16 inches. Using ruler and pastry wheel, trim dough to rectangle exactly 8 × 16 inches. Divide into eight 4-inch squares. Cut each square diagonally from corners to ¾ inch from center. Place 1 teaspoon jam in center of squares. Fold every other corner over filling, pressing lightly on last corner to seal. Transfer pastries to prepared baking sheet. Brush with egg mixture. Repeat with remaining dough. Let rest at room temperature 30 minutes, reglazing once with egg mixture (dough will rise only slightly).

Position rack in center of oven and preheat to 450°F. Reglaze pastries with egg mixture. Transfer pastries to oven and reduce temperature to 400°F. Bake until golden, about 10 to 12 minutes. Cool slightly on wire rack. Meanwhile, mix powdered sugar with 2 tablespoons (or more) hot water until smooth and medium-thick. Drizzle sugar glaze over pastries. Serve warm or at room temperature.

🍎 *Danish Pastry*

The techniques outlined in the recipes on pages 76–80 make the preparation of Danish pastry easy and virtually foolproof. Here are a few additional tips:

- Be sure to keep your dough well chilled at all times: If the butter gets too soft, it will meld into the dough rather than remaining separately layered throughout, causing a loss of flakiness. Don't hesitate to return the dough to the refrigerator to refirm at any point in its making or shaping.

- Note that most of the pastries are baked on a parchment-lined baking sheet. Parchment paper is a good insulator for the bottoms of these fragile pastries, ensuring that they do not overbrown. Also, parchment paper absorbs any butter that may leak out.

- Danish pastries freeze well; pack them carefully in foil or doubled produce-type bags and place them in a protected corner of the freezer. They can be reheated while still frozen—small pastries at 375°F for about 10 minutes, large pastries at 325°F for about 30 minutes. If making and freezing for a future event, apply all glazes after reheating the pastries.

Soon, with practice, your pastries will be a match for the local *pâtisserie*.

Danish Buns

Makes about 40 buns

Filling
- ⅔ cup currants
- ⅔ cup seedless raisins
  Dark rum (about ½ cup)
- ½ cup sugar
- ½ cup firmly packed brown sugar
- 1 tablespoon cinnamon

- 1 recipe Basic Danish Pastry Dough (see recipe, page 78)
- 1 egg beaten with 1 tablespoon milk
- ½ cup sugar crystals*

For filling: Combine currants and raisins in shallow bowl. Add enough rum to cover and let stand for several hours or overnight to plump. Drain well. Combine ½ cup sugar, brown sugar and cinnamon in another small bowl.

Line 2 rimmed baking sheets with parchment paper. Divide dough in half. Return 1 piece to refrigerator. Roll remaining piece out on lightly floured surface into rectangle about 16 × 20 inches. Brush surface with egg mixture. Spread half of sugar mixture over top. Sprinkle with half of currant mixture. Press filling into dough. Starting at long side, roll up dough tightly, pinching to seal. Cut roll into slices 1 inch thick. Transfer to prepared baking sheets, spacing 1 inch apart. Brush with egg mixture. Sprinkle half of sugar crystals evenly over tops. Repeat with second half of dough. Let rest at room temperature 30 minutes (dough will rise only slightly).

Position rack in center of oven and preheat to 450°F. Transfer pastries to oven and immediately reduce temperature to 400°F. Bake until golden brown, about 15 minutes. Cool on wire racks. Serve warm or at room temperature.

*Can be purchased in specialty food markets or through bakeries.

🍎

Double Snails with Lemon Curd

Makes 20 pastries

Lemon Curd
- ¾ cup sugar
- ½ cup strained freshly squeezed lemon juice
- 1 teaspoon cornstarch mixed with 1 teaspoon water
- 2 eggs, well beaten
- 2 tablespoons (¼ stick) butter
- ½ teaspoon finely grated lemon peel

- 1 recipe Basic Danish Pastry Dough (see recipe, page 78)

- 1 egg beaten with 1 tablespoon milk

- 1 cup powdered sugar
- 2 tablespoons whipping cream or milk (about)
- 1 tablespoon strained freshly squeezed lemon juice

For lemon curd: Combine sugar, ½ cup lemon juice and cornstarch mixture in heavy medium saucepan and bring to boil over medium-low heat, whisking constantly. Remove from heat. Whisk ¼ cup hot sugar mixture into eggs in slow steady stream. Gradually whisk egg mixture back into remaining sugar mixture. Cook 2 minutes over medium heat, stirring constantly; *do not boil or mixture will curdle.* Remove from heat and stir in butter and lemon peel. Set saucepan in ice water and cool lemon curd to room temperature, stirring occasionally.

Line 2 rimmed baking sheets with parchment paper. Divide dough in half. Return 1 piece to refrigerator. Roll remaining piece out on lightly floured surface to form rectangle slightly larger than 7½ × 21 inches. Using ruler and pastry wheel, trim dough to rectangle exactly 7½ × 21 inches. Cut rectangle into ten ¾ × 21-inch strips. Twist 1 strip 6 to 8 times. Arrange strip in "U" on work surface, spacing ends about 4 inches apart. Holding ends in place with 1 hand, pick up bottom of "U" and make *double* twist in center of "U," forming ring at bottom. Holding 1 end in each hand, pull ends up and toward you, positioning double twist over center of bottom ring. Tuck ends under and up through holes on each side of double twist. Transfer to prepared baking sheet. Repeat with remaining strips. Brush with egg mixture. Repeat process with second half of dough. Let rest at room temperature 30 minutes (dough will rise only slightly).

Position rack in center of oven and preheat to 450°F. Press down in center of each side of pastries with thumb to form 2 indentations and fill in any remaining holes. Place 1 teaspoon lemon curd into each indentation. Reglaze outer edge of pastries with egg mixture. Transfer pastries to oven and immediately reduce temperature to 400°F. Bake until golden brown, about 20 to 25 minutes (cover loosely with aluminum foil after 10 to 15 minutes if pastries brown too quickly). Transfer pastries to wire rack and let cool slightly, about 5 minutes.

Meanwhile, sift powdered sugar into small bowl. Add 1 tablespoon cream or milk and 1 tablespoon lemon juice and beat until mixture is smooth and medium-thick, adding remaining 1 tablespoon cream or milk as necessary. Drizzle glaze over pastries. Serve warm or at room temperature.

Apple Strudel

Strudel can be assembled 1 day ahead, brushed with melted butter and refrigerated. When butter is firm, cover completely with plastic wrap. Bake up to 8 hours ahead of serving and store at room temperature. Reheat in 300°F oven until warm, about 10 to 15 minutes. Freezing is not recommended.

Makes 1 large or 2 smaller strudels (12 to 16 servings)

¾ cup sugar
½ cup coarsely chopped toasted walnuts
½ cup golden raisins, plumped in wine, drained
1½ teaspoons cinnamon

2 pounds greening or pippin apples
2 tablespoons fresh lemon juice

1 pound phyllo pastry sheets
1 pound unsalted butter, melted
1½ to 2 cups finely ground hazelnuts, pecans, walnuts, almonds, or combination

Powdered sugar

Combine sugar, walnuts, raisins and cinnamon in small bowl; set aside.

Peel, core and thinly slice or coarsely grate apples into large bowl. Sprinkle with lemon juice and toss thoroughly to mix. Add raisin mixture and combine gently but thoroughly. Taste and add more sugar if apples are too tart.

Preheat oven to 375°F. Brush phyllo with melted butter, sprinkle with ground nuts and fill and roll according to basic directions (see box, pages 82–83). Place on greased jelly roll pan or baking sheet with sides and brush with melted butter. Bake 10 minutes. Remove from oven, brush with melted butter, cut into 1½-inch diagonal slices and brush again with melted butter. Push slices together to reshape loaf. Return to oven and continue baking about 30 minutes, brushing every 10 minutes with additional melted butter, until crisp and golden brown. Let cool slightly and serve warm with powdered sugar.

Cheese Strudels with Cherry Glaze

Makes about 4 strudels

Cheese Filling
1 pound cream cheese, room temperature
3 tablespoons sugar
2 tablespoons all purpose flour
2 eggs, lightly beaten
¼ teaspoon cinnamon
⅓ cup raisins (preferably golden)

1 recipe Basic Croissant Dough (see recipe, page 70), ready for shaping
1 egg beaten with 1 tablespoon milk

¼ cup cherry preserves
Sour cream

Combine cream cheese, sugar, flour, eggs and cinnamon in medium bowl and mix well. Stir in raisins. Set aside.

Divide dough into 4 pieces. Return 3 pieces to refrigerator. Roll remaining dough out on lightly floured surface to 6 × 16-inch rectangle. Using pastry bag or spoon, pipe or spread ¾-inch strip of cheese filling across long side of rectangle 1 inch from closest edge. Roll dough up to encase filling, sealing edges firmly. Transfer roll seam side down to ungreased rimmed baking sheet. Brush with egg mixture. Repeat with remaining dough.

Set strudels aside, uncovered, and let rise until doubled in volume, about 1½ hours; reglaze once during rising.

Position rack in center of oven and preheat to 450°F. Reglaze strudels. Transfer baking sheet to oven and immediately reduce temperature to 400°F. Bake until golden brown, about 15 minutes. Immediately transfer to racks.

Strain cherry preserves through sieve set over small saucepan. Place saucepan over medium heat and bring to boil. Brush tops of rolls with cherry glaze. Cut strudels into 1½- to 2-inch sections. Serve immediately or let cool on rack. Pass sour cream separately.

🍒 Steps to a Perfect Strudel Roll

1. Dampen a dish towel, spread it on the counter, and cover it with waxed paper. Unfold the phyllo leaves and set them on top of the waxed paper. Fold the towel, waxed paper and phyllo leaves in half like a book.

2. Consider the towel the book cover, the waxed paper the inside cover and the phyllo leaves the pages of the book.

3. Start opening the "book." Turn to the first "page" (the first phyllo leaf) and brush it with melted unsalted butter (about ½ pound per strudel), then sprinkle lightly with breadcrumbs or nuts.

4. Turn to the next page of phyllo, brush with more melted butter and sprinkle with breadcrumbs; repeat this procedure on each page until you get to the center of the book. Close the book.

5. Starting from the back cover of the book, repeat the process going backwards to the center, brushing each page with butter and sprinkling with breadcrumbs.

6. The book is now open at the center fold. Spread a strudel filling on this center area, being careful to arrange it on the lower third of the page so the strudel can be easily rolled.

7. Tuck in the ends at the left and right ends of the book.

8. Roll the strudel jelly roll-fashion, using the towel and waxed paper to help you roll it. Place the strudel seam side down on an ungreased baking sheet. Brush the top with melted butter. Strudel may be assembled ahead after it has been rolled and brushed with butter. Refrigerate until butter is firm, then cover. Uncover and bring to room temperature before baking.

   Strudel can also be frozen at this stage. Place in freezer and allow butter to firm, then cover with freezerproof wrap. Defrost 30 minutes before baking. Increase baking time slightly. Strudel should be crisp and golden brown.

9. Baking: Preheat the oven according to recipe. Bake 10 to 15 minutes, then remove from the oven and brush again with melted butter. Slice the strudel roll at this point when it is partially baked.

Apricot-Raisin Strudel

Makes 3 strudels

1 cup (2 sticks) butter, cut into pieces (room temperature)	3 tablespoons cinnamon
1 cup (½ pint) vanilla ice cream, softened	⅔ cup apricot preserves
	1 cup cornflake crumbs
2 cups all purpose flour	1 cup chopped nuts
	1 cup golden raisins
3 tablespoons sugar	Milk

Combine butter and ice cream in medium bowl and mix well. Add flour and blend until smooth. Form dough into ball. Wrap in waxed paper or plastic wrap and refrigerate overnight.

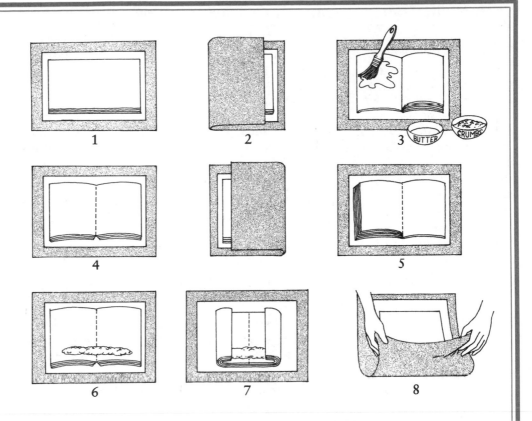

With a serrated-blade knife, carefully cut on the diagonal into 1½-inch slices. Use a seesaw motion so the strudel does not fall apart. Press the slices back together so it looks like one long roll. Return to oven, bake for an additional 15 minutes (25 minutes total baking time), or as recipe suggests.

10. If pastry looks dry while it is baking, brush with melted butter or with the butter that has oozed out onto the baking sheet. Upon removing from the oven, brush again with butter. Arrange sliced strudel on long platter.

Preheat oven to 350°F. Grease baking sheet. Combine sugar and cinnamon in small bowl and set aside. Divide dough into thirds. Roll one portion out on lightly floured surface into rectangle ⅛ inch thick. Spread some preserves evenly over surface. Sprinkle some crumbs, sugar mixture, nuts and raisins over top. Roll up lengthwise as for jelly roll. Repeat with remaining dough.

Brush tops with milk and sprinkle with any remaining sugar mixture. Bake until crisp and golden, about 25 to 30 minutes. Slice strudels diagonally, but do not cut through. Let cool completely on wire rack. Slice through and serve. Store in airtight containers.

Cornets with Béchamel and Goat Cheese Filling

These hors d'oeuvre horns of plenty are small enough for finger food, but longer pastry strips can be used if they are to be served as a first course. Pastry cornets can be made several days ahead and refrigerated baked or unbaked, filled or unfilled; or they can be made several weeks ahead and frozen filled or unfilled. The filling can also be made several days ahead and refrigerated when cool.

12 servings

Pâte Brisée
2⅔ cups all purpose flour
  ½ teaspoon sugar
  ¼ teaspoon salt
  9 ounces (2¼ sticks) cold butter, cut into small pieces
  1 tablespoon lard, cut into small pieces
  9 tablespoons ice water

Béchamel and Goat Cheese Filling
  5 tablespoons butter
  5 tablespoons flour
1½ cups milk
  ¾ cup whipping cream
  3 eggs, lightly beaten
  6 ounces chèvre (goat) cheese, crumbled (¾ cup)
1¼ teaspoons salt
  ½ teaspoon freshly ground pepper
  ½ teaspoon freshly grated nutmeg

  3 tablespoons freshly grated Parmesan cheese

For pâte brisée: Combine flour, sugar and salt in mixing bowl. Add butter and lard and mix with fingertips until mixture resembles grated Parmesan cheese. Add water and mix just until ingredients form ball. Using heel of hand, do a *fraisage* (smear dough out in straight line on work surface). Repeat fraisage. Wrap in waxed paper and let rest in refrigerator at least 1 hour.

For cornets: Generously grease baking sheet and cornet molds or foil molds (see end of recipe). Divide dough in half; refrigerate one piece. Roll remainder into 8 × 18-inch rectangle. Trim edges with fluted pastry wheel. Cut pastry into eighteen 8-inch strips each about ¾ to 1 inch wide. Wrap each strip around mold in overlapping spiral pattern resembling small horn. Place drop of water on end of strip and press into dough to seal. Stand cornets upright or place sealed side down on baking sheet. Repeat with remaining dough. Refrigerate cornets for at least 30 minutes.

Preheat oven to 425°F. Bake cornets 15 minutes. Reduce heat to 350°F and bake until cornets are golden brown, about 10 minutes. Cool in molds on rack 15 minutes. Gently slip off molds and return cornets to rack until cool.

For filling: Melt butter in heavy saucepan over low heat. Whisk in flour and let foam 3 minutes without coloring, stirring constantly. Whisk in milk and cream and stir over medium-high heat until sauce comes to boil. Reduce heat and simmer 15 minutes. Slowly stir sauce into beaten eggs. Return to saucepan, set over medium-high heat and bring to boil, stirring constantly. Add cheese and season to taste with salt, pepper and nutmeg. Cover sauce with plastic wrap if not using immediately.

Preheat oven to 425°F. Using spoon or pastry bag fitted with ½-inch plain tip, fill cornets with béchamel. Return to greased baking sheet and sprinkle ends with Parmesan cheese. (If not serving immediately, cover with plastic wrap and leave at room temperature up to 2 hours.) Bake until pastries are heated through, about 7 minutes.

A half cup of minced ham or prosciutto can be added to filling for variation.

Cornet molds can be purchased from cookware stores or made from aluminum foil. To make 2 cornet molds: Take 12-inch length of aluminum foil, fold diagonally into triangle, then cut triangle in half. Form each double thickness half into cornet (just as you would form paper pastry bag) by placing triangle in front of you with longest side on top. Keeping your finger in center of longest side, take one end and fold down and around into cone so end lines up with tip. Fold other end down and line up with tip to complete cone. Staple edges together to secure. Generously grease each cone before using.

4 ❦ Vegetable Side Dishes

There is certainly nothing wrong with hash-brown potatoes and grilled tomatoes. But it is sometimes impossible to avoid the impression that they are the *only* vegetables that can legally be served in the morning hours. Far from it, as this chapter should indicate. For while vegetables are indispensable as flavorings for omelets, crepes and breads, they are the star attractions in a variety of side dishes that will add interest to—and help balance—almost any brunch or breakfast menu.

Hash browns aside, potatoes are an excellent way to help start the day, and they may appear in any number of guises: mixed with fresh corn, for example, for a simple gratin; as delicate *gnocchi,* served with a fennel sauce and Parmesan cheese; in a peppery sauté, a Mexican version of Potatoes O'Brien that is great with poached eggs; or combined with winter vegetables in a chartreuse, a molded casserole that Carême—who called the chartreuse "the queen of entrées"—would have applauded. Risotto e Funghi (page 88)—arborio rice and mushrooms enhanced by Romano cheese and Marsala—and a down-home version of cheese grits, perfect for Kentucky Derby day or any day, are especially adaptable for lively morning entertaining.

Cold vegetable dishes have a dual appeal: They refresh the palate and add color to the table. Salads are especially appropriate for brunch, and a selection of vegetable-flavored sorbets—cucumber, carrot-dill, avocado-lime, and tomato-ginger—are both beautiful and delicious.

Cream cheese–vegetable spreads add a savory touch to any meal; for something to spread them on, see the previous chapter.

Casseroles and Sautés

Potato and Corn Gratin

4 to 6 servings

2 pounds baking potatoes (8 medium), peeled and sliced into thin rounds
Salt and freshly ground white pepper
4 medium ears corn, grated (about 1 cup)

5 tablespoons butter, cut into small pieces
2 cups buttermilk
2 tablespoons minced fresh chives or green onion (optional garnish)

Preheat oven to 375°F. Generously butter 9 × 12-inch gratin or other baking dish. Arrange half of potato slices in single layer in bottom, overlapping slightly. Season with salt and pepper. Sprinkle with ½ cup corn and dot with 2½ tablespoons butter. Repeat layering. Pour buttermilk over. Bake until milk is absorbed and potatoes are browned and crusty, about 1 to 1¼ hours. Sprinkle with minced chives or green onion and serve immediately.

Potato Gnocchi and Fennel Gratin

This marvelously fennel-flavored gnocchi can be cooked and sauced, then left at room temperature for several hours before baking.

4 servings

8 ounces young fennel or endive
2 tablespoons (¼ stick) butter
1 large shallot, minced
¾ cup whipping cream
Salt and freshly ground pepper

1½ pounds boiling potatoes, unpeeled
1 cup all purpose flour
1½ teaspoons salt

¼ teaspoon freshly ground pepper
⅛ teaspoon freshly grated nutmeg

2½ quarts water
Salt

1½ ounces (½ cup) freshly grated Parmesan cheese
1½ tablespoons butter

Discard tough outer leaves from fennel and remove strings. Slice fennel into julienne, reserving 1½ tablespoons minced fronds for garnish. Melt 2 tablespoons butter in large heavy skillet over low heat. Add fennel and shallot, cover and let sweat, stirring occasionally, until tender, about 30 minutes. Puree in processor or blender with cream. Season to taste with salt and pepper.

Steam potatoes until tender when pierced with knife. Push potatoes through sieve with mallet using straight up and down motion to prevent their becoming glutinous. Working as little as possible, knead in flour, salt, pepper and nutmeg. Roll gnocchi into cylinders 1 inch wide; slice into pieces ¼ inch thick. Press top of each piece lightly with floured fork, then make indentation in center with handle of fork, curling gnocchi up around it.

Preheat oven to 425°F. Butter large gratin pan or casserole dish. Bring water to boil with salt in Dutch oven or large saucepan. Add ⅓ of gnocchi to pan, stirring gently to prevent sticking. After about 3 minutes, gnocchi will float to surface. Wait 10 seconds, then remove from pan using slotted spoon and transfer to prepared dish, arranging in single layer. Repeat with remaining gnocchi.

Pour fennel sauce over gnocchi. Sprinkle with Parmesan and dot with remaining butter. Bake until golden, about 15 minutes. Garnish with reserved minced fennel fronds.

Chartreuse of Winter Vegetables

The chartreuse can be assembled the day before it is baked. If not at room temperature, allow additional baking time. It can also be formed in individual pint molds, such as onion soup bowls. Cooking time will be less.

4 to 6 servings

1 large cabbage (1¾ to 2¼ pounds), cored

1½ pounds boiling potatoes, peeled and quartered

1 tablespoon butter

¼ pound bacon (5 thin slices), blanched in boiling water 3 minutes

1½ pounds turnips, peeled and cut into 1-inch pieces

¼ cup beef stock

2 tablespoons (¼ stick) butter

1 large leek, white part only, thinly sliced (1¾ to 2 cups)

⅓ cup whipping cream

2 egg yolks

¼ teaspoon freshly grated nutmeg
Salt and freshly ground pepper

Blanch cabbage core side down in large pot of boiling salted water until leaves can be separated from head, about 5 minutes. Return half of leaves to water and blanch 10 minutes. Transfer to colander using tongs or slotted spoon. Repeat with remaining cabbage.

Add potatoes to cabbage cooking water and boil until tender. Drain well. Push through sieve using mallet, pressing with straight up and down motion to prevent their becoming glutinous. Transfer to large bowl and set aside.

Melt 1 tablespoon butter in heavy large skillet over low heat. Add bacon and cook until crisp and brown. Cool; crumble and add to potatoes.

Add turnips to same skillet. Cover and cook over heat 5 minutes. Stir; cook 5 minutes longer. Add stock and bring to simmer, scraping up any browned particles clinging to bottom of pan. Cover and braise, stirring occasionally, until turnips are tender when pierced with knife, about 40 minutes. Puree turnips and juices in blender or processor. Sieve into potatoes.

Melt remaining butter in another heavy skillet over low heat. Add leek, cover and cook, stirring occasionally, 20 minutes. Stir into potatoes with cream, egg yolks, nutmeg, salt and pepper.

Preheat oven to 400°F. Butter 3-quart soufflé dish or charlotte mold. Cut out remaining core from cabbage leaves. Pat leaves dry. Sprinkle with salt and pepper. Using ¾ of leaves, line dish with curved part of leaves facing toward center. Place half of potato mixture in mold. Cover with half of remaining cabbage leaves. Top with second half of potato mixture and cover with remaining cabbage leaves.

Cover chartreuse with buttered parchment or foil and bake 20 minutes. Reduce oven temperature to 350°F and continue baking until heated through and skewer inserted into center of mold is hot, about 1 hour and 40 minutes. Let rest 5 minutes. Run knife around edge of mold and turn out onto platter.

The Governor's Cheese Grits

6 servings

1 cup uncooked quick-cooking grits

⅓ pound cheddar cheese, shredded

½ cup (1 stick) butter

2 eggs, lightly beaten

2 garlic cloves, minced

1 teaspoon salt
Pinch of freshly ground white pepper
Pinch of freshly grated nutmeg

Preheat oven to 350°F. Grease 9-inch square baking dish. Cook grits according to package directions. Remove from heat. Add cheese and butter and stir until melted. Blend in eggs and seasonings. Transfer to prepared dish. Bake until set, 25 to 30 minutes.

Risotto e Funghi (Risotto with Mushrooms)

8 to 10 appetizer servings

5 tablespoons unsalted butter
1 small white onion, diced
1½ cups Italian (arborio) rice
½ cup Marsala or dry white wine

1 quart (4 cups) chicken stock
3 saffron pistils

⅓ cup Italian olive oil
4 garlic cloves, minced

1 pound fresh mushrooms, coarsely sliced
Salt and freshly ground pepper

¼ cup freshly grated Romano cheese
Additional Romano cheese

Melt 3 tablespoons butter in heavy 2- or 3-quart saucepan over medium heat. Add onion and cook until golden. Stir in rice and mix until evenly coated with butter. Pour in wine and cook, stirring frequently, until almost evaporated.

Meanwhile, combine chicken stock and saffron in 1½- or 2-quart saucepan and bring to gentle simmer.

Add 1 cup stock to rice and let simmer slowly, stirring occasionally, until liquid is absorbed. Repeat, adding remaining stock 1 cup at a time, and cook until rice is tender (this will take about 30 minutes; toward end of cooking, stirring must be constant or rice will stick).

As stock begins to be absorbed, heat olive oil and garlic in large skillet over medium heat. Add mushrooms, season with salt and pepper and stir frequently until all moisture has evaporated.

As soon as rice is tender, stir in remaining 2 tablespoons butter and ¼ cup Romano, then blend in mushrooms. Serve with additional cheese.

Pepper-Potato Sauté

Potatoes O'Brien with a Mexican twist. Top with poached eggs for brunch.

6 to 8 servings

6 tablespoons (or more) light olive oil
2½ pounds new potatoes, peeled and cut into ½-inch cubes, parboiled 5 minutes and drained
2 medium onions, chopped

2 large sweet red peppers, seeded and cut into ½-inch squares
½ teaspoon salt
⅛ teaspoon freshly ground black pepper

2 teaspoons dried basil or 2 tablespoons minced fresh basil
1 garlic clove, minced
3 tablespoons minced fresh parsley
1 large firm-ripe avocado, peeled, seeded and coarsely chopped
Juice of 1 lime
Salt and freshly ground pepper

Heat oil in large heavy skillet over medium-high heat until hot. Add potatoes and onion and cook about 3 to 4 minutes, stirring often.

Increase heat to high and add peppers (and additional oil if pan seems dry). Continue cooking, scraping up browned bits that cling to bottom of pan. When potatoes take on even golden color, add salt, pepper, basil and garlic. Cook another minute. Remove from heat and gently stir in parsley, avocado, lime juice and salt and pepper to taste. Serve immediately.

Mediterranean Tart

Clockwise from left: *Almond Combs;*
Kathleen McLean's Apricot Pastry; Danish Buns;
Strawberry Pinwheels; Double Snails with Lemon Curd

Savarin with Blueberries

Michel Tcherevkoff

Summer Compote

Irwin Horowitz

Apple Strudel

Salads, Sorbets and Spreads

Poached Leeks in Sauce Verte

Serve with thinly sliced black bread and a bowl of unsalted butter.

6 servings

Sauce Verte
- 2 eggs
- 1 egg yolk
- 1 tablespoon Dijon mustard
- 2 teaspoons white wine vinegar
- ¾ to 1 cup peanut oil
- ½ cup watercress leaves, blanched, drained and chopped
- 2 to 4 tablespoons finely minced fresh parsley (preferably Italian)
- 2 to 3 tablespoons cooked, drained, squeezed and chopped spinach

- 2 to 3 tablespoons finely minced fresh dill
- 2 to 3 tablespoons finely minced fresh chives
  Salt and freshly ground white pepper

- 12 leeks

- 12 slices ham (preferably smoked)
  Cherry tomatoes and parsley sprigs (garnish)

For sauce: Combine first 4 ingredients in processor or blender and mix until smooth. With machine running, slowly add oil in thin steady stream until mixture resembles mayonnaise. Add next 5 ingredients with salt and pepper to taste and mix until smooth. Cover and chill until ready to serve.

Trim leeks, leaving 2 to 3 inches of greens. Carefully slit outer layer and remove; wash and set aside. Slit remaining layers lengthwise (leaving leeks intact) and wash thoroughly. Rewrap in outer layer and tie with string. Let stand in ice cold water 30 minutes.

Drain leeks well. Arrange in single layer in large saucepan. Add water to cover and season with salt. Bring just to boil over high heat. Reduce heat and simmer until leeks are just tender. Drain on paper towels. Carefully remove string.

Wrap each leek with ham and arrange seam side down on rectangular serving platter. Spoon sauce evenly over top. Garnish with tomatoes and parsley.

Snow Pea and White Corn Salad

6 servings

- 1 pound fresh snow peas (strings discarded), cut diagonally into ¼-inch strips
- 6 small ears of sweet corn (preferably white), scraped and blanched

- 1 shallot, chopped
- 2 tablespoons coarsely ground French mustard (Moutarde de Meaux)
- 2 tablespoons cider vinegar

- 9 fresh tarragon leaves or ⅛ teaspoon dried tarragon, crumbled
- 5 fresh mint leaves
- 2 medium-size fresh basil leaves or generous pinch of dried basil, crumbled
  Pinch of sugar
- 6 tablespoons peanut oil
  Salt and freshly ground pepper
- 4 or 5 whole snow peas (garnish)

Place sliced snow peas in colander and pour boiling water over. Drain well; immediately plunge into ice water and drain again. Transfer to container. Mix in corn and set aside.

Combine shallot, mustard, vinegar, tarragon, mint, basil and sugar in processor or blender and mix until smooth. With machine running, gradually add oil in slow steady stream until mixture is creamy. Season with salt and pepper. Pour over vegetables and mix gently. Cover and refrigerate 4 hours, or overnight. Garnish with whole peas.

Sliced Cucumber with Sour Cream

6 servings

1 large English cucumber (18 ounces), peeled, scored and thinly sliced
½ teaspoon salt

½ cup sour cream
Freshly ground pepper
2 teaspoons freshly snipped chives

Place cucumbers in colander and sprinkle with salt. Let stand 30 minutes. Drain well and pat dry with paper towels. Transfer to bowl and add sour cream, pepper and additional salt if necessary. Sprinkle chives over top.

Cucumber Sorbet

Serve this sorbet in cucumber cups made by hollowing out 2-inch segments of unpeeled cucumber, leaving ¼-inch base. Fill with scoops of sorbet, sprinkle lightly with minced fresh basil and garnish with watercress leaves.

Makes 1 quart

⅔ cup sugar
⅔ cup water

3 quarts water
1 tablespoon salt
4 large English (hothouse) cucumbers, peeled, seeded and sliced

¼ cup plus 2 tablespoons cider vinegar
6 medium shallots, minced
½ teaspoon salt

Combine sugar and ⅔ cup water in small saucepan over medium-high heat and stir until sugar is dissolved. Just before syrup comes to boil, remove from heat. Cool, then cover and chill.

Combine remaining water and salt in large saucepan and bring to rapid boil. Add cucumber slices and poach 30 seconds. Drain well and plunge into cold water to stop cooking process. Drain again and pat dry with paper towels. Transfer to food processor or food mill and puree. Combine with vinegar, shallots and salt and blend well. Chill. Stir in syrup. Finish in either ice cream maker or freezer.

Tomato-Ginger Sorbet

Spoon this sorbet into hollowed-out tomato halves and top with a dollop of crème fraîche, or serve over cucumber slices that have been marinated in a tangy Ginger Vinaigrette.

Makes 1 quart

⅔ cup sugar
⅔ cup water

8 medium tomatoes, peeled, seeded and juiced, pureed
3 tablespoons tomato paste
1 cup good quality tomato juice
¼ cup cider vinegar
1 tablespoon chopped Pickled Fresh Ginger (see following recipe)

1 teaspoon salt
3 drops hot pepper sauce
Pinch of cinnamon
Pinch of freshly grated nutmeg
Tomato cups or cucumber slices marinated in Ginger Vinaigrette (see following recipe)

Combine sugar and water in small saucepan over medium-high heat and stir until sugar is dissolved. Just before syrup comes to boil, remove from heat. Allow to cool, then cover and chill.

Simmer tomatoes and tomato paste in medium saucepan until reduced to 2 cups, about 20 minutes. Transfer to mixing bowl. Add tomato juice, vinegar, pickled ginger, salt, hot pepper sauce, cinnamon and nutmeg and blend well. Chill. Add syrup and blend well. Finish in ice cream maker or freezer. Serve in tomato cups or over cucumbers marinated in Ginger Vinaigrette.

Jean Delaveyne's Pickled Fresh Ginger

Pickled ginger can be stored in airtight container in refrigerator several weeks.

3 ounces fresh ginger, peeled and thinly sliced	½ cup plus 2 tablespoons sugar
	½ cup red wine vinegar

Combine all ingredients in small saucepan and bring to boil. Remove from heat. Cool slightly, then cover and chill.

Ginger Vinaigrette

¾ cup oil (preferably safflower oil mixed with 1 tablespoon French olive oil)	2 tablespoons sugar
	1 teaspoon Dijon mustard
¼ cup red wine vinegar	1 teaspoon salt
1 tablespoon ginger pickling liquid (from preceding recipe)	Freshly ground pepper

Combine all ingredients in small bowl or jar with tight-fitting lid and whisk or shake until they are well blended.

Carrot-Dill Sorbet

For a colorful presentation, serve this sorbet in small green pepper halves.

Makes 1 quart

⅔ cup sugar	2 tablespoons frozen orange juice concentrate
⅔ cup water	
1 pound carrots, cooked, drained, pureed and chilled	1 tablespoon Scotch
	1 teaspoon dried dillweed
¼ cup fresh lemon juice	Pinch of salt

Combine sugar and water in small saucepan over medium-high heat and stir until sugar is dissolved. Just before syrup comes to boil, remove from heat. Cool and chill. Add syrup to remaining ingredients and blend well. Finish in either ice cream maker or freezer.

Avocado-Lime Sorbet

Hollowed-out lime halves garnished with mint are the perfect "dishes" for this sorbet, whether served as dessert or palate refresher.

Makes about 3¼ cups

⅔ cup sugar	Drop of hot pepper sauce
⅔ cup water	Pinch of salt
2 large ripe avocados, peeled and pureed	
¼ cup fresh lime juice	

Combine sugar and water in small saucepan over medium-high heat and stir until sugar is dissolved. Just before syrup comes to a boil, remove from heat. Cool slightly, then cover and chill.

Beat avocado with lime juice until completely smooth. Add pepper sauce and salt and blend well. Chill. Stir in syrup. Finish in ice cream maker or freezer.

Savory Walnut Cream Cheese

Makes about 1½ cups

1 cup kefir cheese
¼ cup honey
½ cup cream cheese, room temperature

⅓ cup finely chopped walnuts

Combine kefir cheese and honey in small bowl. Add cream cheese and beat until smooth. Stir in chopped walnuts. Refrigerate until ready to serve.

Whipped Scallion Cream Cheese

Makes about 1½ cups

8 ounces cream cheese, room temperature
1 tablespoon milk (do not use if preparing in food processor)

1 small scallion (½ ounce), minced
Dash of hot pepper sauce

Beat cream cheese until soft and fluffy. Add milk, scallion and hot pepper sauce and blend well. Spoon into 1½-cup serving dish or crock. Cover tightly and chill thoroughly before serving.

5 ❦ Sweet Side Dishes

When cooks are planning a breakfast or brunch, the word *dessert* seldom comes up. It just doesn't seem appropriate, at least as a separate and final course. But sweet dishes definitely have a place in the morning menu; and for most people, a day that starts without a hint of sweetness—even if only in the form of preserves spread on toast—simply isn't right.

Fruits, of course, are a major part of most morning meals. Their natural sweetness can be enhanced, as in such dishes as cinnamon-rich apple slices; an old-fashioned blueberry grunt (not a fish, just another name for dumplings); an Italian zabaglione with figs, honey and Port (this one is *very* sweet); melon in wine; or grilled oranges with prunes. Or, you might prefer fruits in their natural glory, as part of a compote, perhaps.

Cool and refreshing, sorbets add an unusual twist to breakfast or brunch and are especially welcome warm-weather treats. Almost any fruit can be transformed into a delicious sorbet, and when served in pretty glasses, it makes an elegant alternative to fruit juice.

Sweet spreads and sauces are as essential to a good breakfast or brunch as well-brewed coffee and tea, and the offerings are not limited to jams and marmalades. Try honey butter, sweetened cream cheese spreads, fruit sauces and several versions of that most delicate of custard sauces, crème anglaise. Any one can transform an ordinary dish into an extraordinary one with a minimum of effort.

You do not have to be a philosopher to understand why "sugar" and "honey" are terms of endearment—just leaf through the following pages.

 Fruits

Blueberry Grunt

Can be topped with heavy cream and a sprinkling of cinnamon-sugar.

6 servings

Grunts (dumplings)
1 egg
⅓ cup whipping cream
⅔ cup all purpose flour
2 tablespoons sugar
1 teaspoon baking powder
¼ teaspoon salt

Blueberries
½ cup sugar
½ cup water

2 tablespoons fresh lemon juice
½ teaspoon ground allspice
2 pints fresh blueberries, washed and stemmed or 2 12-ounce packages or 1 1½-pound bag frozen, thawed

For grunts: Beat egg with cream in small bowl. Whisk in remaining ingredients to make heavy batter.

For berries: Combine sugar, water, lemon juice and allspice in 11- or 12-inch frying pan and bring to boil. Add blueberries and reduce to *bare simmer*.

Drop *rounded* tablespoons of batter over blueberries, leaving ½ inch between each (there should be 12 to 14 dumplings). Cover and simmer gently *without peeking* 15 minutes. Uncover and test for doneness: Grunts should have risen like mushroom caps and blueberries should be reduced to a sauce. If wooden toothpick inserted into grunts does not come out clean, cover and steam another 5 minutes. Serve in dessert bowls, allowing 2 dumplings per serving.

Apricot Fantasy

6 servings

1 10½-ounce can apricot halves, drained
2 tablespoons unflavored gelatin
1 12-ounce can apricot nectar
½ cup water
1 3⅝-ounce package vanilla pudding mix

1½ to 2 teaspoons fresh lemon juice
1 cup whipping cream, whipped
1 cup fresh strawberries or ½ cup chopped toasted pecans (garnish)

Mash apricot halves in small bowl and set aside. Combine gelatin and ¼ cup nectar in large bowl, stirring until gelatin is dissolved. Blend remaining nectar with ½ cup water in small bowl. Prepare pudding mix according to package instructions, substituting nectar-water mixture for milk. Add hot pudding to gelatin mixture in thin stream, stirring constantly. Add apricots and lemon juice and mix thoroughly. Let cool slightly. Gently fold in whipped cream. Turn apricot mixture into 1-quart soufflé dish or spoon into 6 wine goblets. Cover and refrigerate until set, at least 30 minutes. Garnish with berries or pecans.

Sautéed Cinnamon Apples

8 servings

6 tablespoons (¾ stick) butter
6 Greening or pippin apples, peeled, cored and sliced

2½ tablespoons vanilla sugar mixed with ⅛ to ¼ teaspoon cinnamon

Melt butter in large skillet over medium heat. Add apples, sprinkle with vanilla sugar mixture and sauté, turning carefully with spatula, until delicately browned. Serve immediately.

Port and Honey Zabaglione with Figs

4 servings

12 to 16 fresh figs, peeled
½ cup Port

6 egg yolks

3 tablespoons honey
1½ teaspoons vanilla
¾ teaspoon fresh lemon juice

Make a slit in each fig with sharp knife. Combine figs and Port in large bowl and let stand several hours or overnight, turning occasionally.

Drain Port into measuring cup and add more Port as necessary so liquid measures ½ cup. Arrange figs in individual goblets and set aside.

Combine Port, egg yolks, honey, vanilla and lemon juice in top of double boiler set over simmering water and whisk until mixture thickens and triples in volume (scraping down sides and bottom of pan as you beat), about 5 to 7 minutes; do not let water boil or yolks will curdle. Spoon zabaglione over figs. Serve hot or chilled.

Broiled Grapefruit with Oranges and Port

This morning refresher benefits from being prepared several hours ahead and chilled to allow flavors to mingle.

6 servings

3 large grapefruits, halved
1 small seedless orange, scored and cut into 6 slices
3 tablespoons frozen orange juice concentrate

3 tablespoons light brown sugar (or less if grapefruit is very sweet)
3 tablespoons Port

Cinnamon

Using small, flexible serrated knife, carefully separate grapefruit segments from rind and membranes. Top each grapefruit half with orange slice. Combine concentrate, sugar and Port and blend well. Spread about 1 tablespoon of mixture over each half. *(Can be made in advance to this point and chilled.)*

When ready to serve, preheat broiler. Sprinkle grapefruit with cinnamon. Set halves on baking sheet and broil 5 inches from heat source until edges of grapefruit are lightly browned.

Strawberry-Filled Cantaloupe

2 servings

1½ cups whole strawberries, hulled, rinsed and drained
Sugar
Kirsch or crème de cassis

1 small cantaloupe, halved and seeded

Combine strawberries with sugar and liqueur to taste. Cover and marinate at least 30 minutes. Spoon into cantaloupe and chill until ready to serve.

Tropical Fruit with Lime

2 servings

Fresh mint or geranium leaves
(garnish)
1 papaya, peeled, seeded and cubed

1 mango, peeled, pitted and cubed
Juice of 1 lime
1 lime, cut into wedges (garnish)

Arrange fresh mint or geranium leaves attractively on platter. Top with fruit and sprinkle with lime juice. Chill. Garnish with lime wedges before serving.

Summer Compote with Fresh Lemon Ice Cream

A striking creation for a big summer party. Recipe can easily be halved or quartered for a smaller gathering. Sprinkle each layer of fruit with sugar if sweeter compote is desired. Accompanying Fresh Lemon Ice Cream should be semisoft when served. For fresh lime ice cream, substitute fresh lime juice and lime peel for lemon.

18 to 20 servings

Compote
1 honeydew melon, peeled, seeded and cubed
6 cups (3 pints) fresh strawberries, hulled and halved
2 cups (1 pint) fresh raspberries
6 nectarines, peeled, cubed and tossed with juice of 1 lemon
3 kiwis, peeled and sliced into rounds
6 peaches, peeled, cubed and tossed with juice of 1 lemon
4 navel oranges, peeled and cut into slices ¼ inch thick

3 to 4 cups peeled, seeded and cubed casaba melon
1 bottle Asti Spumante wine
½ cup Grand Marnier
8 sprigs fresh mint (garnish)
8 whole strawberries (garnish)

Fresh Lemon Ice Cream
3½ cups sugar
¾ cup fresh lemon juice
2 tablespoons grated lemon peel
2 quarts (8 cups) whipping cream
¼ teaspoon salt

For compote: Arrange honeydew melon in bottom of 5- to 6-quart straight-sided glass bowl. Place strawberry halves cut side out around sides of bowl. Fill center with raspberries. Top with nectarines. Arrange kiwi rounds around sides of bowl above strawberry halves. Fill center with peaches. Place orange slices around sides of bowl above kiwi. Fill center with casaba. Pour in Asti Spumante and Grand Marnier. Garnish top of compote with alternating sprigs of mint and whole berries. Cover and chill about 8 hours.

For ice cream: Combine sugar, lemon juice and peel in large freezer container. Slowly stir in cream and salt, blending well. Cover and freeze until firm outside but still soft in center; stir through several times. Freeze until firm.

Scoop into glass bowl set in larger bowl of ice and serve with compote.

Oranges Orientale

6 servings

Zest (peel) of 2 oranges, removed in long thin strips with zester or grater
2 tablespoons sugar
2 tablespoons orange juice

1 tablespoon Grand Marnier
6 large seedless oranges (rind and pith removed), cut into ⅛-inch slices

Gently mix zest, sugar, orange juice and liqueur. Pour over orange slices, cover tightly and chill at least 1 hour, preferably overnight. Let stand at room temperature at least 20 minutes before serving. Arrange in shallow dish or orange halves, spooning sauce over top.

Melon in Sweet Wine

6 servings

½ small ripe cantaloupe, seeded
¼ ripe honeydew melon, seeded
¼ ripe casaba melon, seeded

1 cup sweet white wine (Barsac, Sauternes or Anjou)
1 teaspoon minced candied ginger

Scoop out melon balls using 1-inch diameter melon baller (you should have about 1¼ cups of each). Transfer to 4- to 5-cup container. Add wine and ginger and mix well. Cover and refrigerate overnight. To serve, arrange fruit on dessert plates and spoon liquid over.

Grilled Autumn Oranges and Prunes

For a delicious variation, fill prunes with toasted whole almonds.

4 servings

12 pitted dried prunes
¼ cup Grand Marnier
4 large oranges, peeled (all pith removed), very thinly sliced and seeded

½ teaspoon fresh lemon juice

2 to 3 tablespoons sugar
Mint sprigs (garnish)

Combine prunes and Grand Marnier in medium saucepan and bring to boil over medium-high heat, stirring frequently. Remove from heat, cover and let cool 1 hour, stirring occasionally. Transfer to large bowl. Add oranges and mix gently. Let stand several hours or overnight, turning occasionally.

Using slotted spoon, arrange fruit in single layer in large oval or round broilerproof gratin pan or 4 individual pans. Blend lemon juice into liqueur mixture and pour over fruit.

Preheat broiler. Sprinkle fruit with sugar. Broil as close to heat source as possible until fruit browns, about 3 to 5 minutes. Garnish fruit with mint sprigs and serve immediately.

Oat and Coconut Granola

Makes about 3 quarts

5 cups rolled oats
3 cups shredded unsweetened coconut
1 cup coarsely chopped walnuts, pecans or almonds
1 cup raw wheat germ
½ cup sesame seeds

½ cup sunflower seeds
½ teaspoon salt
¾ cup honey
½ cup safflower or corn oil
2 teaspoons vanilla
1 cup chopped dates or raisins

Preheat oven to 350°F. Thoroughly combine first 7 ingredients in large bowl. Heat honey, oil and vanilla in small saucepan. Pour over dry ingredients, stirring to coat well. Mix in dates or raisins. Spread mixture no more than ½ inch deep in shallow baking pan(s). Bake until lightly browned, about 30 minutes, stirring frequently so edges do not overbrown. Cool completely. Store in tightly covered container(s) in refrigerator.

Winter Compote

2 servings

½ cup drained canned apricot halves (packed in water)

½ cup drained canned pitted dark sweet cherries

½ cup drained canned pineapple chunks (packed in own juice)

4 tablespoons dark rum

2 tablespoons orange juice

2 teaspoons brown sugar

Pinch of ground cloves

Pinch of cinnamon

Combine all ingredients except 2 tablespoons rum in medium saucepan and simmer over medium-high heat, stirring frequently, 15 minutes. Transfer to bowl. Heat reserved rum in same saucepan. Pour over fruit and ignite, shaking bowl gently until flame subsides. Serve compote warm.

 # Sorbets

Apple Sorbet

Serve with Strawberry-Raspberry Sauce, or either of the Crèmes Anglaises (see recipes, page 104).

Makes 1 quart

¾ cup sugar

¾ cup water

3 large tart apples (preferably Granny Smith), peeled, cored and pureed

¼ cup fresh lemon juice

2 tablespoons applejack

Pinch of cinnamon

Pinch of nutmeg

Combine sugar and water in small saucepan over medium-high heat and stir until sugar is dissolved. Just before syrup comes to boil, remove from heat. Cool and chill. Add syrup to remaining ingredients and blend well. Finish in either ice cream maker or freezer.

Cantaloupe Sorbet

Makes 1 quart

⅔ cup sugar

⅔ cup water

4 cups chopped ripe cantaloupe, pureed

½ cup Port

2 tablespoons fresh lemon juice

Zest of 1 lemon, minced

Pinch of salt

Pinch of cinnamon

2 tablespoons whipping cream or crème fraîche

Cantaloupe wedges

Combine sugar and water in small saucepan over medium-high heat and stir until sugar is dissolved. Just before syrup comes to boil, remove from heat. Allow to cool, then cover and chill.

Combine syrup, melon, Port, lemon juice, zest, salt and cinnamon and blend well. Place in ice cream maker and freeze partially so sorbet is still soft. Add cream and complete churning. If using conventional freezer, turn mixture into metal container and freeze. Thaw partially, spoon into food processor and beat until smooth and fluffy. Add cream and continue mixing until well blended. Refreeze. Scoop into cantaloupe wedges for serving.

Apricot Sorbet

Hollowed-out pineapple shells or orange halves are natural servers. Serve with Fresh Pineapple Sauce, Crème Anglaise or Orange Crème Anglaise (see recipes, pages 103–104).

Makes 1 quart

⅔ cup sugar
1 cup water

1 cup dried apricots
1 29-ounce can apricot halves, drained and pureed

¼ cup fresh orange juice
1 tablespoon fresh lemon juice
Zest of 1 orange, minced

Combine sugar and ⅔ cup water in small saucepan over medium-high heat and stir until sugar is dissolved. Just before syrup comes to boil, remove from heat. Cool, then cover and chill.

Combine dried apricots and remaining water in small saucepan and bring to boil. Reduce heat and simmer until apricots are softened and water is absorbed, stirring occasionally to prevent burning or scorching. Transfer mixture to food processor, blender or food mill and puree. Combine with pureed apricot halves, orange and lemon juices and zest. Chill. Stir in syrup. Finish in either ice cream maker or freezer.

Cranberry-Pear Sorbet

Makes 1 quart

⅔ cup sugar
⅔ cup water

3 cups fresh or frozen whole cranberries, pureed
2 ripe pears, peeled, cored and pureed

2 tablespoons kirsch
Zest of 2 oranges, minced
1 egg white

Combine sugar and water in small saucepan over medium-high heat and stir until sugar is dissolved. Just before syrup comes to boil, remove from heat. Allow to cool, then cover and chill.

Combine syrup, cranberries, pears, kirsch and zest and blend well. Place in ice cream maker and freeze partially so sorbet is still soft. Add egg white and complete churning. If using conventional freezer, turn mixture into metal container and freeze. Thaw partially, spoon into food processor and beat until smooth and fluffy. Add egg white and continue mixing until well blended. Refreeze mixture before serving.

Banana Sorbet

Serve with Strawberry-Raspberry Sauce, Orange Crème Anglaise or Pineapple Sauce (see recipes, pages 103–104).

Makes 1 quart

⅔ cup sugar
⅔ cup water
1 cup fresh orange juice

2 large firm ripe bananas, pureed
2 tablespoons dark rum
1 tablespoon fresh lemon juice

Combine sugar and water in small saucepan over medium-high heat and stir until sugar is dissolved. Just before syrup comes to boil, remove from heat. Cool and chill. Add syrup to remaining ingredients and blend well. Finish in either ice cream maker or freezer.

🍒 Basic Sorbet Techniques

Sorbets, which are French sherbets, are frozen purées of fruits or vegetables. Related to ice cream, they are distinguished by their small amount—or absence—of cream. In making sorbets, follow these techniques:

- The syrup ratio: equal portions of water and sugar. Use ⅔ cup water and ⅔ cup sugar for 1 cup syrup. Make a large quantity at one time; it stores indefinitely in refrigerator.
- Formula is 3 cups puree to 1 cup syrup or 2 cups juice to 2 cups syrup, with only a few exceptions.
- Egg white, whipping cream, crème fraîche or yogurt is added only when necessary for the texture.
- For a desirable consistency, the ingredients for a sorbet must be chilled before mixing and freezing.
- Sorbets may be frozen in either an ice cream maker or in the freezer. If frozen in the freezer without a special machine, they must be placed in a metal container (an 8-inch layer cake pan is ideal for 1 quart) for fast freezing. They are also prepared in two steps. This differs from the one-step preparation in the ice cream machine. After they are frozen, they must be partially thawed, then beaten in a food processor using the steel knife. The egg white, whipping cream, crème fraîche or yogurt is added in this second process.
- Sorbets that have become crystalline in the freezer should be partially thawed, then reprocessed in the food processor using the steel knife, or beaten with a wooden spoon, and refrozen. They should be made as needed, preferably within 24 hours.
- Store in airtight plastic containers.
- One hour before serving, remove from freezer and place in refrigerator for optimum flavor and texture.

Sorbets may be frozen in an ice cream maker or in the freezer. When using the latter method, complete the sorbet by partially thawing and then beating in the food processor until smooth and fluffy. Refreeze until served.

Lemon Sorbet

This sorbet is especially attractive served in hollowed-out lemon, lime or orange halves; or small scoops may be placed on scored lemon or orange slices.

Makes 1 quart

1 cup sugar
1 cup water

2 to 2¼ cups fresh lemon juice

Zest of 3 lemons, minced
2 egg whites

Combine sugar and water in small saucepan over medium-high heat and stir until sugar is dissolved. Just before mixture comes to boil, remove from heat. Cool slightly, then cover and chill.

Combine syrup, lemon juice and zest and blend well. Place in ice cream maker and freeze partially so sorbet is still soft. Add egg whites and complete churning. If using conventional freezer, turn mixture into metal container and freeze. Thaw partially, spoon into food processor and beat until smooth and fluffy. Add egg whites and continue mixing until well blended. Refreeze.

Lime Marmalade Sorbet

Hollowed-out lime halves are perfect for individual portions. Garnish with fresh mint leaves for an extra tingle. Serve with Crème Anglaise (see recipe, page 104).

Makes about 3½ cups

1 large or 2 small limes, quartered
1⅓ cups sugar
1½ cups water
1 tablespoon fresh lime juice

2 tablespoons fresh lemon juice
1 egg white

Combine limes in small saucepan with water to cover and boil slowly until tender, about 10 minutes. Drain. Combine limes and ⅓ cup sugar in food processor or blender and mix well. With machine running, slowly add ½ cup water. Transfer to saucepan and simmer slowly until thick, about 25 minutes. Remove marmalade from heat and stir in lime juice. Set aside.

Combine remaining sugar and water in small saucepan over medium-high heat and stir until sugar is dissolved. Just before syrup comes to boil, remove from heat. Cool, then cover and chill.

Combine syrup, marmalade and lemon juice and blend well. Place in ice cream maker and freeze partially so sorbet is still soft. Add egg white and complete churning. If using conventional freezer, turn mixture into metal container and freeze. Thaw partially, spoon into food processor and beat until smooth and fluffy. Add egg white and continue mixing until well blended. Refreeze.

Orange Sorbet

Makes 1 quart

1 cup sugar
1 cup water

2 large oranges
½ cup frozen orange juice concentrate

½ cup fresh lemon juice
2 tablespoons whipping cream or crème fraîche

Combine sugar and water in small saucepan over medium-high heat and stir until sugar is dissolved. Just before syrup comes to boil, remove from heat. Allow to cool, then cover and chill.

Remove zest from oranges and mince. Remove and discard rind and pith. Cut oranges into quarters and puree in food processor or blender. Combine syrup, puree, zest, concentrate and lemon juice and blend well. Place in ice cream maker and freeze partially so sorbet is still soft. Add cream and complete churning. If using conventional freezer, turn mixture into metal container and freeze. Thaw partially, spoon into food processor and beat until smooth and fluffy. Add cream and continue mixing until well blended. Refreeze.

Purple Plum-Prune Sorbet

Serve with Crème Anglaise (see recipe, page 104) flavored with 2 tablespoons of ruby Port.

Makes 1 quart

⅔ cup sugar
⅔ cup water

10 pitted prunes
½ cup Port

2 17-ounce cans purple plums, drained, pitted and pureed
¾ cup fresh orange juice
Zest of 1 orange, minced

Combine sugar and water in small saucepan over medium-high heat and stir until sugar is dissolved. Just before syrup comes to boil, remove from heat. Allow to cool, then cover and chill.

Combine prunes and Port in small saucepan over high heat and bring to boil. Reduce heat and simmer 10 minutes until softened. Transfer to food processor or blender and puree. Chill.

Add syrup and puree to remaining ingredients and blend well. Finish in either ice cream maker or freezer.

Fresh Strawberry Sorbet

Serve with Crème Anglaise, Orange Crème Anglaise or Strawberry-Raspberry Sauce (see recipes, pages 103–104).

Makes 1 quart

⅔ cup sugar
⅔ cup water
2½ pints ripe strawberries, pureed and chilled

2 tablespoons Grand Marnier
2 tablespoons fresh lemon juice
Minced kiwi slices or sliced strawberries (garnish)

Combine sugar and water in small saucepan over medium-high heat and stir until sugar is dissolved. Just before syrup comes to boil, remove from heat. Cool and chill. Add syrup to remaining ingredients except garnish and blend well. Finish in ice cream maker or freezer. Garnish with kiwi or strawberries (mix berries gently with sugar and additional Grand Marnier if desired).

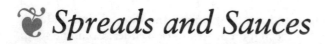 *Spreads and Sauces*

Dried Apricot Jam

Makes about 8 half-pint jars

1½ pounds dried apricots, quartered
2 quarts water

4 pounds sugar

2 ounces blanched, halved almonds
Juice of 1 large lemon

Rinse apricots. Combine with water in medium bowl. Cover and let stand at room temperature for 48 hours.

Prepare jars. Turn undrained apricots into Dutch oven or other large kettle and bring slowly to boil. Add sugar and stir until dissolved. Let boil until apricots are plump and mixture is thick, about 40 minutes to 1 hour, adding nuts and lemon juice during last 10 minutes of cooking time. Pour jam into hot sterilized jars to within ¼ inch of top and seal. Process 5 minutes in boiling water bath. Remove from water and let stand undisturbed until cooled. Test for seal. Store in cool dark place.

Peach Jam

Makes 3 half-pint jars

5 cups peeled, chopped ripe peaches
(about 3 pounds)
Juice of 1 large lemon

3 cups sugar
2 teaspoons orange flower water

Prepare jars. Combine peaches and lemon juice in Dutch oven or large kettle and simmer gently until peaches are soft. Add sugar and stir until dissolved. Increase heat to high and bring to hard boil. Let boil until setting point is reached, about 15 minutes. Stir in orange flower water and boil another minute. Skim foam from surface. Pour jam into sterilized jars to within ¼ inch from top and seal. Process 5 minutes in boiling water bath. Remove from water and let stand undisturbed until cooled. Test for seal. Store in cool dark place.

Lime Marmalade

Marmalade is a delicious preserve easily made at home. To ensure success, the simmered fruit should be boiled with sugar just to the setting point. If it is cooked too long, the result will be a thick syrup with hard chunks of peel. The Scots add a nip of brandy at the end of cooking to heighten flavor.

Makes about 4 half-pint jars

1¼ pounds limes (about 9 limes)
3½ cups water

4½ cups sugar

Chill a small plate. Prepare jars. Wash limes. Carefully remove peel and cut into very fine shreds. Remove pith and membrane and place in washed cheesecloth or muslin. Thinly slice limes and remove pits *(you need 2 cups sliced fruit)*; add pits to cheesecloth and tie securely. Combine sliced lime, peel, cheesecloth bag and water in heavy large saucepan and bring to boil. Reduce heat and simmer mixture about 1½ hours.

Remove bag, squeezing liquid into pan before discarding. Add sugar, stirring until dissolved. Increase heat and bring to hard boil. Let boil until setting point is reached, about 15 minutes. Remove from heat. Spoon small amount onto chilled plate and refrigerate. If it stiffens after 1 minute, it is done; if not, return to boil briefly and test again. Pour into hot sterilized jars to within ¼ inch of top and seal. Process 5 minutes in boiling water bath. Remove from water and let stand undisturbed until cooled. Test for seal. Store in cool dark place.

Strawberry-Raspberry Sauce

Serve with the sorbets on pages 98–102.

Makes 2 cups

1 pint strawberries, hulled
1 10-ounce package frozen
raspberries, thawed and drained

1 tablespoon kirsch

Combine all ingredients (reserve several strawberries for garnish) and puree. Transfer to serving dish, slice remaining strawberries and gently stir into sauce.

Fresh Pineapple Sauce

Serve with the sorbets on pages 98–102.

Makes 1⅓ cups

¼ fresh pineapple, cored and cut
into chunks
¼ cup sugar

2 tablespoons dark rum
1 tablespoon fresh lime or lemon
juice

Puree pineapple until smooth. Add remaining ingredients and blend well.

Crème Anglaise

Serve with the sorbets on pages 98–102.

Makes about 2 cups

7 egg yolks
½ cup sugar
Pinch of salt

2 cups milk
1 1-inch piece vanilla bean, split and scraped

Combine yolks, sugar and salt and beat until thick and light in color, about 1 minute. Scald milk with vanilla bean in nonaluminum pan. Remove vanilla bean and set aside. Slowly beat 1 cup milk into yolk mixture. Gradually return mixture to milk in saucepan, whisking constantly. Add vanilla bean and cook over medium heat, stirring constantly, until mixture thickens; *do not boil.* Strain custard if necessary. Pour into metal bowl set in cold water or ice and cool, stirring occasionally. Refrigerate. *Custard will thicken as it cools.*

Orange Crème Anglaise

Serve with the sorbets on pages 98–102.

Makes about 2 cups

7 egg yolks
½ cup sugar
Pinch of salt

2 cups milk
Zest of 1 orange, minced
2 teaspoons fresh orange juice

Combine yolks, sugar and salt and beat until thick and light in color, about 1 minute. Scald milk in nonaluminum saucepan. Slowly beat 1 cup milk into yolk mixture. Gradually return mixture to milk in saucepan, whisking constantly. Add zest and juice and continue cooking over medium heat, stirring constantly, until mixture thickens; *do not boil.* Strain custard into metal bowl set in cold water or ice and cool, stirring occasionally. Cover and refrigerate. *Custard will thicken as it cools.*

Whipped Honey Butter

Makes ¾ cup

½ cup (1 stick) unsalted butter, room temperature

¼ cup honey

Beat butter in bowl with hand mixer or spoon until creamy and light. Add honey and whip until fluffy. Cover and refrigerate. Bring honey butter to room temperature before serving.

For variation, add finely chopped lemon peel or grated orange peel.

Orange Peel Cream Cheese

Makes about 1 cup

½ cup cream cheese, room temperature
3 tablespoons unsalted butter, room temperature

2 tablespoons fresh orange juice
1 tablespoon (or more) honey
1 tablespoon grated orange peel
1 teaspoon fresh lemon juice

Combine all ingredients in blender and mix until just blended. Taste and adjust flavor, adding more honey if sweeter spread is desired. Cover and refrigerate until ready to serve.

6 ❦ Beverages

There was a time—and not so long ago—when the choice of breakfast beverages was limited, to say the least. Only three questions were likely to be asked: Do you want your coffee black or with cream? One lump or two? And do you want orange juice or something exotic, like tomato juice? Any deviation from the norm was frowned upon. People who requested tea, for example, were looked at askance; they were possibly foreign, and certainly a little eccentric.

But the increased sophistication of tastes brought change. The coffee grinder is now standard kitchen equipment, and the beans that go into it come from as far away as Indonesia and Kenya. Fresh tea leaves from the East have replaced the once-ubiquitous teabag in many homes. And with the great popularity of brunch as a major weekend meal, a choice between orange and tomato juice is simply no longer enough: Brunch menus cry out for variety, and some of that new variety is explored in this chapter.

Dairy drinks, of course, provide a refreshing start to the day. Based on milk, yogurt or buttermilk and flavored with fruit and vegetable juices and other ingredients, they are nutritious, easy to make and great crowd pleasers—especially when kids are part of the crowd.

More spirited beverages—hot and cold punches and cocktails, including variations on the Bloody Mary, the Margarita and the traditional navy grog, are sure to enliven any morning. But the favorite morning beverage, coffee, is still too good to overlook, and makes a delicious base for blended drinks as well as an incomparable concoction all on its own.

While the choice of breakfast and brunch beverages is now virtually limitless, there is still one hard-and-fast rule: Make a lot.

🍒 Juices and Dairy Drinks

Apricot Nectar Cooler

Makes 1 cup

½ cup apricot nectar, chilled
½ cup plain yogurt

¼ teaspoon fresh lemon juice
Mint sprig (garnish)

Combine nectar, yogurt and lemon juice in blender and mix well. Pour into chilled glass and garnish with mint.

If thicker drink is desired, freeze apricot nectar until almost firm before combining with remaining ingredients.

Banana Cooler

Makes ¾ cup

½ large ripe banana
½ cup buttermilk (chilled) or plain yogurt

½ teaspoon light honey
¼ teaspoon fresh lemon juice
Lemon slice (garnish)

Combine banana, buttermilk or yogurt, honey and lemon juice in blender and mix well. Pour into chilled glass and garnish with lemon slice.

Melon Cooler

Makes 1¼ cups

1 cup peeled ripe melon cubes (cantaloupe, honeydew, casaba, Persian or Crenshaw)
½ cup buttermilk (chilled) or plain yogurt

1 teaspoon light honey
½ to 1 teaspoon fresh lemon juice
½ teaspoon grated lemon peel
2 to 3 melon balls threaded on skewer (garnish)

Combine melon cubes, buttermilk or yogurt, honey, lemon juice and peel in blender and mix well. Pour into chilled glass. Garnish with skewered melon.

Tomato Ice

2 servings

3 large tomatoes, peeled, seeded and chopped
¼ cup chopped onion
¼ cup chopped celery
1 tablespoon sugar
1 tablespoon fresh lemon juice
½ teaspoon Worcestershire sauce
¼ teaspoon salt

2 sprigs fresh mint or ¼ teaspoon dried, crumbled
2 to 3 drops hot pepper sauce
1 small garlic clove, crushed

Mint sprigs (garnish)

Combine all ingredients except garnish in processor or blender and puree until smooth. Taste and adjust seasoning (mixture should be highly seasoned as freezing tends to diminish flavor). Pour into shallow container and freeze.

Spoon mixture into processor or blender and mix until fluffy (or transfer to medium bowl and beat with electric mixer). Return to container, cover and freeze until firm. Just before serving, divide between two wine glasses and garnish with mint sprigs.

Buttermilk and Fruit Smoothie

Make sure the fruit has been chilled overnight.

2 servings

2 cups fresh berries
2 cups buttermilk

1 small banana, cut into chunks
1 to 2 tablespoons honey

Combine all ingredients in blender and mix until smooth. Serve immediately.

Orange Juice Cooler

Makes about 1¼ cups

1 cup buttermilk (chilled) or plain yogurt
3 tablespoons frozen orange juice concentrate

Orange slice (garnish)

Combine buttermilk or yogurt and orange juice concentrate in blender and mix well. Pour into chilled glass and garnish with orange slice.

Lassi (Yogurt Drink)

6 to 8 servings

1 quart (4 cups) plain yogurt
2 tablespoons almonds
2 tablespoons sugar or honey or to taste

1 cup ice cubes
Rose water

Combine 1 cup yogurt with nuts and sugar in blender and mix at high speed until nuts are pulverized. Add ice cubes and remaining yogurt and blend again at high speed. Pour into glasses and sprinkle with few drops of rose water.

Cold Punches and Cocktails

Clam Bloody Mary

Makes 12 servings

1 6½-ounce can minced clams, undrained
4 large green onions (2 ounces total), minced
1 16-ounce can tomatoes, undrained
1 46-ounce can tomato juice
2 8-ounce bottles clam juice

2 tablespoons fresh lemon juice
1½ teaspoons Worcestershire sauce
6 drops hot pepper sauce or to taste
Salt and freshly ground pepper
1½ cups (12 ounces) vodka or to taste
Additional tomato juice (if cocktail requires thinning)

Puree clams with liquid in processor or blender. Transfer to 3-quart pitcher (preferably glass); stir in onion. Cut tomatoes crosswise and remove seeds. Puree with liquid in processor or blender. Add to pitcher with remaining ingredients except vodka and additional tomato juice. Adjust seasoning. Refrigerate at least 2 hours or overnight. Just before serving, add vodka, and tomato juice if needed.

Margarita Punch

Makes about fifty 4-ounce servings

3 quarts tequila
4 cups (1 quart) Triple Sec
2 cups fresh lemon juice
2 cups fresh lime juice
Block of ice

2 quarts club soda
Coarse salt
Fresh lime wedges

Combine tequila, Triple Sec, lemon juice and lime juice in large bowl, blending well. Refrigerate. Shortly before serving, place block of ice in large punch bowl. Add tequila mixture and soda and stir gently until blended. Pour salt into saucer. Run lime wedges around rims of punch cups, then press rims into salt. Ladle punch into salt-rimmed cups and serve.

South Seas Punch

Makes about fifty 4-ounce servings

4 750-ml bottles Riesling or Rhine wine
1½ quarts light brown rum
1½ cups fresh lemon or lime juice
1½ cups curaçao
1½ cups pineapple juice
Block of ice

4 cups (1 quart) club soda
Pineapple slices (garnish)
1 cup flaked fresh coconut (optional garnish)

Combine wine, rum, lemon or lime juice, curaçao and pineapple juice in large bowl, blending well. Refrigerate. Shortly before serving, place block of ice in large punch bowl. Add wine mixture and club soda and stir gently until blended. Float pineapple slices over top. Sprinkle each serving with flaked fresh coconut if desired.

Sangría

Makes about 4⅔ cups

1 fifth (about 3¼ cups) dry Burgundy
⅔ cup fresh lemon juice
½ cup sugar

¼ cup freshly squeezed orange juice
Ice cubes
Lemon and orange slices (garnish)

Combine first 4 ingredients in large pitcher. Fill wine glasses with ice. Pour sangría into glasses and garnish each with lemon and orange slices.

Coconut Blizzard

12 servings

2 16-ounce cans sliced pineapple, drained
4 cups plain yogurt
2 8-ounce cans cream of coconut
1 cup dark rum
2 tablespoons sugar
6 to 8 ice cubes

Using half of ingredients at a time, combine in processor or blender until smooth and creamy. Serve in chilled daiquiri-type glasses.

Rum and Pineapple Fizz

4 servings

1 8-ounce can unsweetened pineapple chunks, drained
1 cup crushed ice
4 ounces (½ cup) dark rum
1 egg white
1 ounce (2 tablespoons) fresh lemon juice
1 ounce (2 tablespoons) fresh lime juice
1 tablespoon sugar
Chilled club soda

Combine all ingredients except soda in blender and mix at low speed 15 seconds or until ice is thoroughly blended. Divide mixture among 4 wine glasses (preferably with 8- or 9-ounce capacity). Top each glass with soda and stir lightly.

Nat's Grog

4 to 6 servings

1 6-ounce can frozen guava juice concentrate or 1 12-ounce can guava nectar
2 cups crushed ice
1 cup Jamaica rum punch
2 ounces (¼ cup) orange liqueur
Juice of 1 lemon
½ teaspoon allspice
Ice cubes

Combine all ingredients except ice cubes in blender and mix until smooth. Pour over ice and serve immediately.

🍇 *Hot Drinks*

English Hot Rum Punch

Makes about fifty 4-ounce servings

4 cups (1 quart) Barbados or other good quality medium rum
1 750-ml bottle Cognac or brandy
1 cup fresh lemon juice
1 cup firmly packed brown sugar
9 whole cloves
3 quarts boiling water
50 twists of lemon peel (garnish)

Combine rum, Cognac or brandy, lemon juice, brown sugar and cloves in warmed punch bowl and stir until sugar dissolves. Add boiling water and blend well. Ladle into mugs. Garnish each serving with lemon peel.

🍎 *All about Coffee*

Coffee beans—not beans at all but the pit of a cherrylike fruit from an evergreen tree—come from many parts of the world. From Central and South America, in addition to Brazil's enormous crop (used mostly for blending), there are mellow Colombian, mild Costa Rican and richly aromatic Antiguan from Guatemala. From East and West Africa, connoisseurs search out rich, clean-tasting Kenyan and exotic Ethiopian. Indonesia produces Java (a name that has long been synonymous with fine coffee) and fine Celebes Kalossi. The West Indies trees contribute, among others, Jamaican Blue Mountain, a coffee as rare as a Vermeer. The only coffee produced in the United States is the Kona variety, grown on the slopes of Hawaiian volcanoes.

Most coffee is made from two varieties of beans: the aristocratic *arabica,* which is grown at high altitudes and produces all the finest coffees, and the blander *robusta,* used mostly for instant coffees and for blending. Both start out as nondescript green beans whose appearance belies the aromatic secrets exposed when the heat in the roasting process causes them to expand like popcorn kernels, changing their color and bringing their flavor to the surface.

Trial by fire in a roasting machine produces roasts from the lightest cinnamon color through the darkest espresso. In *The Signet Book of Coffee and Tea,* Peter Quimme says that full city roast is the ideal one, its chestnut color confirming that the beans are at the maximum development of their rich, genuine flavor. Darker roast coffees range from Viennese through French and almost black Italian, which has the strongest flavor and slightly less caffeine than lighter roasts. If you're in search of a caffeine-free coffee, try decaffeinated Colombian or French roasts, which have the same flavor as their kickier siblings but have been freed, by means of a chemical or organic solvent, of the physiological effects of caffeine.

To make the perfect cup of coffee, whether from commercially vacuum-packaged coffee or freshly ground beans bought at a specialty store, you must follow certain rules. First, match the grind to the method: Percolators use regular grind, automatic electric drip and filter cones take drip, vacuum coffee makers a fine grind and espresso pots a very fine grind. Always use two level tablespoons of coffee to six ounces of freshly drawn cold water newly brought to the boil (the only exception is in double-strength coffees such as *café filtre*

British Navy Punch

Can also be served cold.

Makes about thirty-six 4-ounce servings

8 cups (2 quarts) freshly brewed strong hot tea
2 cups sugar
1 750-ml bottle brandy
1 750-ml bottle dark Jamaican rum
1 cup fresh lemon juice
Lemon slices (garnish)

Combine tea and sugar in large saucepan over medium heat and bring to boil, stirring until sugar is dissolved. Transfer to punch bowl. Stir in brandy, rum and lemon juice. Garnish with lemon slices. Serve hot.

and espresso, and for them you use twice as much coffee). Too much coffee makes a bitter brew, too little a weak one, so if you think your coffee is too strong, dilute it with hot water after brewing or try a lighter roast.

The best way to make coffee is with the quick and easy drip method, while the ubiquitous American percolator wins the prize for making the absolute worst. It either boils the coffee or fails to heat it enough or extends the eight-minute brewing cycle, extracting oils mercilessly from the beans and producing a bitter parboiled liquid. Other methods that produce a good cup of coffee include vacuum pots, plunger pots like the French Melior, cold water steeping, which produces a concentrate, or espresso machines. The pot must be absolutely clean since oils and residues can affect the brewing. Don't use a large pot to make small amounts and do serve the coffee immediately.

No matter how careful your preparation and how fine your machine, it will all be for nothing if the beans or ground coffee aren't fresh. Once beans are roasted, most retain their freshness for only about three weeks: Darker French and Italian roasts have a somewhat longer life. Once ground, all beans begin to lose their flavor immediately and are at their best for only four or five days. Unopened vacuum-packed coffee stays fresh for months; once the can is opened, the same figures apply. For the freshest coffee, either buy ground coffee in small quantities or grind the beans at home as you need them. Store beans in an airtight canister at room temperature or in an airtight glass jar with rubber seal in the refrigerator or freezer.

Then all you need is some cold water and expectant taste buds as you set off on the adventure of finding coffees you like. A clear, clean-flavored blend containing Colombian is a favorite choice of many for breakfast; Kona, Brazilian Santos, East African and Central American are other preferred varieties. In the evening, the dark-roasted French and Italian coffees are popular.

Don't be afraid to experiment in the wonderland of beans and blends. Americans are known to have the biggest coffee habit in the world, so you might as well uphold the national average of 2.06 cups a day with blends that please you. No matter what, it is unlikely that your consumption will match Voltaire's 72 cups a day, or that your cup will equal the "bathtub-sized" one favored by Teddy Roosevelt—who spoke softly and carried a big mug.

The Bishop

This simple mull is marked by a rich purple color known as bishop's violet.

4 servings

1 orange
12 cloves
1 fifth dry red wine

1 cinnamon stick
½ cup sugar

Stud orange with cloves and simmer with wine and cinnamon stick in medium saucepan 30 minutes. Add sugar and stir until dissolved. Serve in preheated mugs.

❦ All about Tea

Whether you are planning an elaborate tea ceremony or just contemplating a simple potful with friends, the varieties of tea are many. But no matter if it is called Darjeeling, Formosa Oolong or Dragon Well, all tea comes from one plant, an evergreen shrub of the camellia family, which grows best in tropical and subtropical climates. Though the plant prefers warm, wet days, it will grow almost anywhere; and tea grown at higher, cooler altitudes, much like high-grown coffees, is often considered the finest by tea connoisseurs.

Despite the many varieties and blends, there are really only three kinds of tea—black, oolong and green. It is the processing that determines their differences. Processing is either a three- or four-step operation. First, *withering* removes as much moisture as possible from the leaves. Then *rolling* breaks up the cell structure of the dried leaves and releases their natural juices and fragrances. Third, *fermentation* (actually a misleading technical term for the process of oxidation) exposes the leaves to air; the oxygen they absorb changes the color of the leaves from green to copper or black. Finally, they are *dried* or *fired,* which stops the oxidation process and dries the leaves evenly.

Black tea, which accounts for almost 97 percent of the tea drunk in the United States, is subjected to all four processing steps. Darjeeling, Keemun and Ceylon are black teas. A well-brewed black tea will have a rich, strong flavor and mellow aroma.

Oolong teas are lightly withered and rolled and only partially fermented before being dried; the leaves are half copper, half black. Not as strong as black tea, oolong is rich and fruity tasting.

Green teas are not fermented. The leaves are steamed or heated rather than withered, then rolled and dried. The leaves remain green because they do not oxidize. Green tea is light and clear with a delicate, flavorful taste.

Black tea is graded by the size of the leaf and divided into classes that are not indicative of flavor or quality. Orange pekoe, which many people mistakenly assume to be a variety of tea, is made up of long, thin black leaves; pekoe, the shorter, not as wiry leaves; and pekoe souchong, the largest, rounded leaves. The whole leaves need a longer brewing time, while the broken leaves (about 80 percent of the crop) make a stronger, darker pot of tea in less time. The broken grades are usually considered the choice teas, especially in the United States where they are the essential tea for tea bags. Green teas are graded according to the style of drying as well as the size of the leaves.

Though processing produces only three types of finished tea, there are in fact dozens of varieties, usually named for the area in which they were grown, and some 3,000 different blends. Each tea has its own style and grace, its own loyal followers and avid supporters.

Keemun, one of the finest black teas China produces, is complex and subtle, just as good wine is, with a powerful aroma and rich taste. Just the tea for an early morning bracer. From China's Fukien province there's Lapsang Souchong, smoky and exotic. Dragon Well, the rarest of China's green teas and one of the legendary teas of the world, is sweet and delicate.

Distinguished Indian teas include rich Darjeeling, the Champagne of teas, grown at the foothills of the Himalayas; and sturdy Assam, a powerful black tea that makes a brisk pungent pot. If you can drink just one oolong, be sure it's Formosa Oolong, picked only once a year in Taiwan. Another rare gem of a tea is Ceylon, blended from the best estates in high growing areas.

Of all the tea varieties, English Breakfast, traditionally a China Keemun, is surely one of the most popular. It got its name from the English habit of adding milk to tea, which brings out its distinctive aroma. Earl Grey, a blend of Indian and Ceylon teas flavored with oil of bergamot, is another popular tea. Legend has it that the recipe for this blend was given to Earl Grey, a British ambassador, by a Chinese mandarin.

Herbal teas, which aren't really teas at all—they don't come from tea plants or have any caffeine—are becoming an increasingly fashionable drink. They are what the French call *tisanes* and are made by pouring boiling water over any variety of dried herbs and spices ranging from verbena, mint leaves, spicy sassafras and astringent rose hips to ginseng, peppermint or soothing camomile. All are said to have beneficial effects—some stimulating, some soothing—on various organs.

One pound of tea makes approximately 200 cups and most tinned teas last only about one year, so when you've decided on a variety worthy of investigation, be careful not to buy more than you need. Fine Keemuns and Darjeelings have the best track record for staying fresh, while green teas lose quality very quickly. Loose teas bought from a specialty shop that has a large volume of business will probably be fresher and keep longer than prepackaged teas. Store in lightproof, airtight containers at room temperature.

Though all the curious tea-brewing paraphernalia available could intimidate the novice, making the perfect cup of tea *shouldn't* be difficult: All you need is a teapot and fresh water. Use a clean porcelain or earthenware teapot that has been warmed by filling with hot water for a few minutes. Put one teaspoon of tea per six-ounce cup into it and bring freshly drawn water to a rolling boil. Pour it over the leaves immediately, let it steep for five minutes and serve. Some experts disapprove of tea balls because the leaves can't expand in the water but remain packed in the ball. And many suggest using distilled or spring water if you're not crazy about the source from your local tap. Tea bags, the invention of a New York merchant who filled small silk bags with portions of tea as tasters' samples, are more expensive than loose tea and rarely contain fine blends. But they can make adequate tea if you leave them to steep for the required five minutes.

It's hardly in the refined British custom of tea with milk and sugar, but tea enthusiasts of experimental bent can try their favorite drink in any number of guises, including the very popular iced version. Sun tea, a product of time and energy, requires only one quart of cold water, ten tea bags and a sunny morning. After six hours or so, your tea will be brewed perfectly and ready to pour over ice for a thirst-quenching reviver. Or try tea ice cream made with English Breakfast tea for a deliciously different treat, then use the leaves for a spot of fortune-telling. It might get you into hot water with tea traditionalists, but then, that's precisely where tea leaves belong.

Cafe Mexicano

2 servings

1½ ounces (1½ squares) semisweet chocolate, broken into pieces
1 cup milk
1 tablespoon sugar
¼ teaspoon almond extract
¼ teaspoon cinnamon
1 cup hot, strong coffee
2 ounces (¼ cup) brandy
2 cinnamon sticks (optional)

Combine chocolate and milk in small saucepan over low heat and cook gently, stirring constantly, just until chocolate melts and milk is hot but not boiling. Transfer to food processor or blender. Add sugar, almond extract and cinnamon and mix 15 seconds. Fill 2 large mugs half full with chocolate mixture. Pour enough hot coffee into each mug to almost fill. Add brandy to each and garnish with cinnamon stick, if desired.

Cafe Maison

A delectable house specialty that evolved after much trial and error.

Makes 12 cups

1 cup plus 1 tablespoon regular roast coffee
½ cup plus 1 tablespoon French roast coffee (the dark espresso-style coffee)
1 tablespoon cocoa
½ to 1 teaspoon ground cinnamon
Water (as designated by coffee pot)

Combine coffees in basket of a drip-style coffee maker or in carafe of French plunger-type pot. Sprinkle cocoa and cinnamon over (do not mix in or you could clog the drain holes). Make coffee as you usually do and serve hot, with or without sugar and cream.

🍎 Index

Almonds
  Almond Combs, 77
  Almond Crumb Loaf, 65
Alsatian Kugelhupf, 74
Apples
  Apple Crepes, 51
  Apple Custard Sauce, 55
  Apple Sorbet, 98
  Apple Strudel, 81
  German Apple Pancake, 52
  Mashed Potatoes with Sorrel and
    Apples, 42
  Pumpkin-Apple Bundt Bread, 62
  Sautéed Apples, 43
  Sautéed Cinnamon Apples, 95
  Scandinavian Apple Cake, 63
Apricots
  Apricot Fantasy, 94
  Apricot Glaze, 73
  Apricot Nectar Cooler, 106
  Apricot-Raisin Strudel, 82
  Apricot Sorbet, 99
  Dried Apricot Jam, 102
  Kathleen McLean's Apricot
    Pastry, 76
Asparagus
  Asparagus and Ham Timbale with
    Hollandaise Sauce, 13
  Asparagus Soup, 10
  Asparagus Tart with Hollandaise
    Sauce, 33
  Asparagus Yogurt Soufflé, 16
Avocado
  Avocado Cream, 36
  Avocado-Lime Sorbet, 91

Bacon
  Baked Egg Custard with Onion
    and Bacon, 19
  Schnitzen (Bacon with Dried
    Fruits and Potatoes), 48
  Spinach and Bacon Tart, 20

Baked Egg Custard with Onion and
  Bacon, 19
Bananas
  Banana Cooler, 106
  Banana Sorbet, 99
  Best-Ever Banana Bread, 63
Basic Danish Pastry Dough, 78
Basic Whole Wheat Danish Pastry
  Dough, 76
Beer and Cheese Soufflé, 14
Bishop, The, 111
Blini, Buckwheat, with Caviar and
  Smoked Salmon, 61
Blintzes, Cheese, A Russian
  Grandma's, 53
Blueberries
  Blueberry Buckle, 66
  Blueberry Grunt, 94
  Savarin with Blueberries, 73
Bockwurst, 45
Bran Muffins, 66
Breads, Quick
  Almond Crumb Loaf, 65
  Best-Ever Banana Bread, 63
  Blueberry Buckle, 66
  Bran Muffins, 66
  Brown Rice Raisin Muffins, 66
  Fig Rum Loaf, 65
  Inverary Inn's Bonnach, 63
  Mocha Yogurt Loaf, 64
  Pumpkin-Apple Bundt Bread, 62
  Rhubarb Nut Bread, 64
  Scandinavian Apple Cake, 63
  Sweet Corn Bread, 64
Breads, Yeast. See also Croissants
  Alsatian Kugelhupf, 74
  Fruit and Marzipan Brioche, 72
  Jane's Sweet Whole Wheat Bread,
    69
  Savarin with Blueberries, 73
  Sourdough English Muffins, 69
  Sourdough Sour Cream Coffee
    Cake, 74

Spiced Dark Bread with Currants,
  67
Walnut Wheat Bread, 68
Yeast Ring with Streusel Topping,
  75
Yogurt Bread Starter, 68
Breakfast Sausages, 42
Brioche, Fruit and Marzipan, 72
British Navy Punch, 110
Broccoli-Cauliflower Pie, 31
Broiled Grapefruit with Oranges
  and Port, 95
Brown Rice Raisin Muffins, 66
Buckwheat Blini with Caviar and
  Smoked Salmon, 61
Buttermilk and Fruit Smoothie, 107

Cafe Maison, 114
Cafe Mexicano, 114
Cantaloupe
  Cantaloupe Sorbet, 98
  Strawberry-Filled Cantaloupe, 95
Carrots
  Carrot-Dill Sorbet, 91
  Cauliflower, Carrot and Parmesan
    Quiche, 32
Casseroles and Sautés
  Governor's Cheese Grits, The, 87
  Pepper-Potato Sauté, 88
  Potato and Corn Gratin, 86
  Potato Gnocchi and Fennel
    Gratin, 86
  Risotto e Funghi (Risotto with
    Mushrooms), 88
Cauliflower
  Broccoli-Cauliflower Pie, 31
  Cauliflower, Carrot and Parmesan
    Quiche, 32
  Cauliflower-Watercress Soufflé
    with Tomato Cream Sauce, 15
Champagne Sausage with Sauce
  Piquante, 43
Chartreuse of Winter Vegetables, 87

Cheese
Beer and Cheese Soufflé, 14
Cauliflower, Carrot and Parmesan
Quiche, 32
Cheese Croissants, 72
Cheese Strudels with Cherry
Glaze, 81
Cornets with Béchamel and Goat
Cheese Filling, 84
Deep-Dish Chili-Cheese Pie, 25
Gibanica (Serbian Cheese Pie), 34
Governor's Cheese Grits, The, 87
Russian Grandma's Cheese
Blintzes, A, 53
Spanakopitta (Spinach, Onion and
Cheese Pie), 26
Cherry Glaze, 81
Chicken
Chicken Breasts Wrapped in
Endive with Herb Butter and
Sauce Chivry, 39
Seared Chicken Livers with
Chives, 38
Chilies
Chili Salsa, 57
Deep-Dish Chili-Cheese Pie, 25
Chorizo, 44
Clam Bloody Mary, 107
Classic Omelet, 7
Cocktails. See Punches and
Cocktails
Coconut Blizzard, 109
Coffee, 110
Cafe Maison, 114
Cafe Mexicano, 114
Cold Poached Salmon with Avocado
Cream, 36
Corn
Potato and Corn Gratin, 86
Potato Corn Pancakes and Chili
Salsa, 57
Sweet Corn Bread, 64
Corned Beef Hash in Baked Potato
Shells with Fresh Tomato Butter
Sauce, 40
Cornets with Béchamel and Goat
Cheese Filling, 84
Cornmeal Beer Crepes, 58
Cornmeal-Chive Pastry, 25
Crabmeat Tart, 27
Cranberry-Pear Sorbet, 99
Cream Cheese
Orange Peel Cream Cheese, 104
Savory Walnut Cream Cheese, 92
Whipped Scallion Cream Cheese,
92
Crème Anglaise, 104
Crème Anglaise, Orange, 104
Crepes. See also Pancakes, Savory
Apple Crepes, 51
Chocolate Crepes, 51
Cornmeal Beer Crepes, 58
folding, 61
general information about
preparation of, 60

Green Herb Crepes, 58
Herb Crepes, 60
Herb Crepes Bernoise, 59
Mediterranean Crepes, 58
Nut Crepes, 58
Savory Crepes, 58
Sweet Crepes with Chocolate
Topping, 51
Croissants. See also Breads, Yeast
Basic Croissants, 70
Cheese Croissants, 72
Petits Pains au Chocolat, 71
Whole Wheat Croissants, 71
Cucumbers
Cucumber Sorbet, 90
Sliced Cucumber with Sour
Cream, 90
Custard Sauce, 66

Dairy Drinks
Buttermilk and Fruit Smoothie,
107
Lassi (Yogurt Drink), 107
Danish Buns, 79
Danish Pastry
Basic Danish Pastry Dough, 78
Basic Whole Wheat Danish Pastry
Dough, 76
techniques for preparation of, 79
Deep-Dish Chili-Cheese Pie, 23
Diamond Jim's Oyster and Spinach
Soufflé, 17
Double Snails with Lemon Curd, 80
Dried Apricot Jam, 102

Eggs. See also Omelets
Asparagus and Ham Timbale with
Hollandaise Sauce, 13
Baked Egg Custard with Onion
and Bacon, 19
Boiled Eggs, 4
French Scrambled Eggs, 10
Frittata Di Zucchine, 13
Huevos en Cazuela, 3
Kentucky Scrambled Eggs, 6
Perfect Eggs Benedict, The, 2
Poached Eggs, 4
Poached Eggs and Creamed
Chard, 4
Tomato-Baked Eggs, 6
Trattoria Eggs, 6
English Hot Rum Punch, 109
English Muffins, Sourdough, 69

Fantasy Quiche, 20
Fig Rum Loaf, 65
Flauta Tart, 25
French Scrambled Eggs, 10
French Toast, Superduper, 55
French Toast with Apple Custard
Sauce, 55
Fresh Lemon Ice Cream, 96
Fresh Pineapple Sauce, 103
Fresh Strawberry Sorbet, 102
Fresh Tomato Butter Sauce, 41

Frittata Di Zucchine (Italian Egg
Pancake with Zucchini), 13
Fruit and Marzipan Brioche, 72
Fruits. See also Juices; Sorbets,
Sweet
Apricot Fantasy, 94
Bacon with Dried Fruits and
Potatoes, 48
Blueberry Buckle, 66
Blueberry Grunt, 94
Broiled Grapefruit with Oranges
and Port, 95
Buttermilk and Fruit Smoothie,
107
Fruit and Marzipan Brioche, 72
Grilled Autumn Oranges and
Prunes, 97
Melon in Sweet Wine, 97
Oat and Coconut Granola, 97
Oranges Orientale, 96
Port and Honey Zabaglione with
Figs, 95
Quiche Alsacienne aux Fruits
(Alsatian Fruit Quiche), 30
Sautéed Cinnamon Apples, 95
Strawberry-Filled Cantaloupe, 95
Summer Compote with Fresh
Lemon Ice Cream, 96
Tourte of Sausage and Winter
Fruits, 23
Tropical Fruit with Lime, 96
Winter Compote, 98

German Apple Pancake, 52
Gibanica (Serbian Cheese Pie), 34
Ginger, Pickled Fresh, 91
Ginger Vinaigrette, 91
Glazed Ham Loaf, 48
Governor's Cheese Grits, The, 87
Granola, Oat and Grapefruit, 97
Grapefruit, Broiled, with Oranges
and Port, 95
Gravlax, 37
Grilled Autumn Oranges and
Prunes, 97

Ham
Glazed Ham Loaf, 48
Tart of Leeks, Ham and Tomato,
21
Herb Crepes, 60
Herb Crepes Bernoise, 59
Hollandaise Sauce, 3, 14, 33
Homemade Sausage Patties, 41
Hot Drinks
Bishop, The, 111
British Navy Punch, 110
Cafe Maison, 114
Cafe Mexicano, 114
Coffee, 110, 114
English Hot Rum Punch, 109
Tea, 112
Huevos en Cazuela, 3

Inverary Inn's Bonnach, 63
Italian Egg Pancake with Zucchini, 13
Italian Rice Pancakes with Spinach Basil Sauce, 56
Italian Sausage, 44

Jane's Sweet Whole Wheat Bread, 69
Juices
    Apricot Nectar Cooler, 106
    Banana Cooler, 106
    Melon Cooler, 106
    Orange Juice Cooler, 107
    Tomato Ice, 106

Kajmak, 34
Kentucky Scrambled Eggs, 6
Kugelhupf, Alsatian, 74

Lassi (Yogurt Drink), 107
Leeks
    Poached Leeks in Sauce Verte, 89
    Tart Of Leek, Ham and Tomato, 21
Lemons
    Fresh Lemon Ice Cream, 96
    Lemon Curd, 80
    Lemon Sorbet, 100
Limes
    Lime Marmalade, 103
    Lime Marmalade Sorbet, 101
Magnolia Hotel's Puffy Pancakes, The, 50
Margarita Punch, 108
Marmalade Soufflé, 19
Mashed Potatoes with Sorrel and Apples, 42
Meats
    Bockwurst, 45
    Breakfast Sausages, 42
    Champagne Sausage with Sauce Piquante, 43
    Chorizo, 44
    Corned Beef Hash in Baked Potato Shells with Fresh Tomato Butter Sauce, 40
    Glazed Ham Loaf, 48
    Homemade Sausage Patties, 41
    Italian Sausage, 44
    Saucisson en Croute, 46
    Schnitzen (Bacon with Dried Fruits and Potatoes), 48
    Tart of Leeks, Ham and Tomato, 21
Mediterranean Tart, 22
Melon Cooler, 106
Melon in Sweet Wine, 97
Mixed Vegetable Terrine with Béchamel and Red Pepper Puree, 11
Mocha Yogurt Loaf, 64
Mousseline Sauce, 18
Mousselines of Potato, Onion and Garlic, 16

Muffins. See Breads, Quick
Mushrooms
    Mushroom Tart, 28
    Risotto e Funghi (Risotto with Mushrooms), 88
Mustard Mayonnaise, 38
Mustard Wine Sauce, 45

Nat's Grog, 109

Oat and Coconut Granola, 97
Oat Waffles, 54
Omelet à la Lyonnaise, 7
Omelets
    Classic Omelet, 7
    Omelet à la Lyonnaise, 7
    Puffy Omelet, 8
    Spanish Garden Omelet Loaf, 10
    Sprout Peanut Omelet, 9
    techniques for preparation of, 9
Onions
    Baked Egg Custard with Onion and Bacon, 19
    Mousselines of Potato, Onion and Garlic, 16
    Spanakopitta (Spinach, Onion and Cheese Pie), 26
    Zewelwai (Onion Pie), 30
    Zucchini-Onion Pancakes Gratinées, 59
Oranges
    Grilled Autumn Oranges and Prunes, 97
    Orange Crème Anglaise, 104
    Orange Juice Cooler, 107
    Orange Nut Waffles with Orange Syrup, 54
    Orange Peel Cream Cheese, 104
    Orange Sorbet, 101
    Orange Syrup, 55
    Oranges Orientale, 96

Pancakes, Savory. See also Crepes
    Buckwheat Blini with Caviar and Smoked Salmon, 61
    Herb Crepes, 60
    Italian Rice Pancakes with Spinach Basil Sauce, 56
    Potato Corn Pancakes and Chili Salsa, 57
    Zucchini-Onion Pancakes Gratinées, 59
Pancakes, Waffles and Toasts
    French Toast with Apple Custard Sauce, 55
    German Apple Pancake, 52
    Magnolia Hotel's Puffy Pancakes, The, 50
    Oat Waffles, 54
    Orange Nut Waffles with Orange Syrup, 54
    Quick Scandinavian Pancake, 51
    Russian Grandma's Cheese Blintzes, A, 53
    Sourdough Pancakes, 50

Superduper French Toast, 55
Sweet Crepes with Chocolate Topping, 51
Pastries
    Almond Combs, 77
    Apple Strudel, 81
    Apricot-Raisin Strudel, 82
    Basic Danish Pastry Dough, 78
    Basic Whole Wheat Danish Pastry Dough, 76
    Cheese Strudels with Cherry Glaze, 81
    Cornets with Béchamel and Goat Cheese Filling, 84
    Danish Buns, 79
    Double Snails with Lemon Curd, 80
    Kathleen McLean's Apricot Pastry, 76
    preparation of, 22
    Strawberry Pinwheels, 78
    Strudel Rolls, preparation of, 82
    Wheat Germ Pastry, 32
    Whole Wheat Short Pastry, 27
Pâte Brisée, 84
Peach Jam, 103
Pears
    Cranberry-Pear Sorbet, 99
Pepper-Potato Sauté, 88
Perfect Eggs Benedict, The, 2
Petits Pains au Chocolat, 71
Pickled Fresh Ginger, 91
Pies
    Broccoli-Cauliflower Pie, 31
    Deep-Dish Chili-Cheese Pie, 25
    Gibanica (Serbian Cheese Pie), 34
    Salmon Pie, 26
    Spanakopitta (Spinach, Onion and Cheese Pie), 26
    Spiced Spinach Pie, 29
    Zewelwai (Onion Pie), 30
Pineapple
    Fresh Pineapple Sauce, 103
    Rum and Pineapple Fizz, 109
Poached Leeks in Sauce Verte, 89
Port and Honey Zabaglione with Figs, 95
Potatoes
    Mashed Potatoes with Sorrel and Apples, 42
    Mousselines of Potato, Onion and Garlic, 16
    Pepper-Potato Sauté, 88
    Potato and Corn Gratin, 86
    Potato Corn Pancakes and Chili Salsa, 57
    Potato Gnocchi and Fennel Gratin, 86
Poultry
    Chicken Breasts Wrapped in Endive with Herb Butter and Sauce Chivry, 39
    Seared Chicken Livers with Chives, 38

Prunes
    Grilled Autumn Oranges and
        Prunes, 97
    Purple Plum-Prune Sorbet, 102
Puff Pastry, 47
Pumpkin-Apple Bundt Bread, 62
Punches and Cocktails
    Clam Bloody Mary, 107
    Coconut Blizzard, 109
    Margarita Punch, 108
    Nat's Grog, 109
    Rum and Pineapple Fizz, 109
    Sangría, 108
    South Seas Punch, 108
Purple Plum-Prune Sorbet, 102

Quiche Alsacienne aux Fruits
    (Alsatian Fruit Quiche), 30
Quiches. See also Tarts
    Cauliflower, Carrot and Parmesan
        Quiche, 32
    Fantasy Quiche, 20
    Quiche Alsacienne aux Fruits
        (Alsatian Fruit Quiche), 30
    Zucchini Quiche, 34
Quick Scandinavian Pancake, 51

Raspberries
    Strawberry-Raspberry Sauce, 103
Rhubarb Nut Bread, 64
Risotto e Funghi (Risotto with
    Mushrooms), 88
Rum
    English Hot Rum Punch, 109
    Fig Rum Loaf, 65
    Rum and Pineapple Fizz, 109
Russian Grandma's Cheese Blintzes,
    A, 53

Salads
    Poached Leeks in Sauce Verte, 89
    Sliced Cucumber with Sour
        Cream, 90
    Snow Pea and White Corn Salad,
        89
Salmon
    Buckwheat Blini with Caviar and
        Smoked Salmon, 61
    Cold Poached Salmon with
        Avocado Cream, 36
    Gravlax, 37
    Salmon Pie, 26
Sangría, 108
Sauce Chivry, 40
Sauce Piquant, 43
Sauces
    Apple Custard Sauce, 55
    Chili Salsa, 57
    Crème Anglaise, 104
    Custard Sauce, 66
    Fresh Pineapple Sauce, 103
    Fresh Tomato Butter Sauce, 41
    Hollandaise Sauce, 3, 14, 33
    Mustard Wine Sauce, 45
    Orange Crème Anglaise, 104

Orange Syrup, 55
    Sauce Chivry, 40
    Sauce Piquante, 43
    Spinach Basil Sauce, 57
    Strawberry-Raspberry Sauce, 103
    Strawberry Yogurt Sauce, 54
    Sweet Mustard Sauce, 38
Saucisson en Croute, 46
Sausage
    Bockwurst, 45
    Breakfast Sausages, 42
    Champagne Sausage, 43
    Chorizo, 44
    Homemade Sausage Patties, 41
    Italian Sausage, 44
    making and cooking, 46
    Saucisson en Croute, 46
    Tomato and Sausage Tart, 22
    Tourte of Sausage and Winter
        Fruits, 23
Sautéed Apples, 43
Sautéed Cinnamon Apples, 95
Savarin with Blueberries, 73
Savory Crepes, 58
Scandinavian Apple Cake, 63
Schnitzen (Bacon with Dried Fruits
    and Potatoes), 48
Seafood
    Cold Poached Salmon with
        Avocado Cream, 36
    Crabmeat Tart, 27
    Diamond Jim's Oyster and
        Spinach Soufflé, 17
    Gravlax, 37
    Salmon Pie, 26
    Seafood Soufflé, 16
    Seafood Strudel, 36
Seared Chicken Livers with Chives,
    38
Serbian Cheese Pie, 34
Sliced Cucumber with Sour Cream,
    90
Snow Pea and White Corn Salad, 89
Sorbets, Savory
    Avocado-Lime Sorbet, 91
    Carrot-Dill Sorbet, 91
    Cucumber Sorbet, 90
    Tomato-Ginger Sorbet, 90
Sorbets, Sweet
    Apple Sorbet, 98
    Apricot Sorbet, 99
    Banana Sorbet, 99
    basic techniques for preparation
        of, 100
    Cantaloupe Sorbet, 98
    Cranberry-Pear Sorbet, 99
    Fresh Strawberry Sorbet, 102
    Lemon Sorbet, 100
    Lime Marmalade Sorbet, 101
    Orange Sorbet, 101
    Purple Plum-Prune Sorbet, 102
Soufflés
    Asparagus Yogurt Soufflé, 16
    Beer and Cheese Soufflé, 14
    Cauliflower-Watercress Soufflé
        with Tomato Cream Sauce, 15

Diamond Jim's Oyster and
        Spinach Soufflé, 17
    Marmalade Soufflé, 19
    Seafood Soufflé, 16
    Sweet Potato Soufflé, 18
Sourdough English Muffins, 69
Sourdough Pancakes, 50
Sourdough Sour Cream Coffee
    Cake, 74
Sourdough Starter, 50, 52
South Seas Punch, 108
Spanakopitta (Spinach, Onion and
    Cheese Pie), 26
Spanish Garden Omelet Loaf, 10
Spiced Dark Bread with Currants,
    67
Spinach
    Diamond Jim's Oyster and
        Spinach Soufflé, 17
    Italian Rice Pancakes with
        Spinach Basil Sauce, 56
    Spanakopitta (Spinach, Onion and
        Cheese Pie), 26
    Spiced Spinach Pie, 29
    Spinach and Bacon Tart, 20
    Spinach Turban, 12
Spreads
    Dried Apricot Jam, 102
    Lime Marmalade, 103
    Mustard Mayonnaise, 38
    Peach Jam, 103
    Savory Walnut Cream Cheese, 92
    Whipped Honey Butter, 104
    Whipped Scallion Cream Cheese,
        92
Sprout Peanut Omelet, 9
Strawberries
    Fresh Strawberry Sorbet, 102
    Strawberry-Filled Cantaloupe, 95
    Strawberry Pinwheels, 78
    Strawberry-Raspberry Sauce, 103
    Strawberry Yogurt Sauce, 54
Strudel rolls, preparation of, 82
Strudels. See Pastries
Summer Compote with Fresh
    Lemon Ice Cream, 96
Superduper French Toast, 55
Sweet Corn Bread, 64
Sweet Crepes with Chocolate
    Topping, 51
Sweet Mustard Sauce, 38
Sweet Potato Soufflé, 18

Tart of Leeks, Ham and Tomato, 21
Tarts. See also Quiches
    Asparagus Tart with Hollandaise
        Sauce, 33
    Crabmeat Tart, 27
    Flauta Tart, 24
    Mediterranean Tart, 24
    Mushroom Tart, 28
    Spinach and Bacon Tart, 20
    Tart of Leeks, Ham and Tomato,
        21
    Tomato and Sausage Tart, 22

Tourte of Sausage and Winter Fruits, 23
Tea, 112
Toasts. *See* Pancakes, Waffles and Toasts
Tomatoes
  Fresh Tomato Butter Sauce, 41
  Tart of Leek, Ham and Tomato, 21
  Tomato and Sausage Tart, 25
  Tomato-Baked Eggs, 6
  Tomato Cream Sauce, 15
  Tomato-Ginger Sorbet, 90
  Tomato Ice, 106
Tourte of Sausage and Winter Fruits, 24

Trattoria Eggs, 6
Tropical Fruit with Lime, 96

Vegetables. *See individual vegetables*
Vegetables, mixed
  Chartreuse of Winter Vegetables, 87
  Mixed Vegetable Terrine with Béchamel and Red Pepper Puree, 11

Waffles. *See* Pancakes, Waffles and Toasts
Walnut Wheat Bread, 68
Wheat Germ Pastry, 32
Whipped Honey Butter, 104
Whole Wheat Bread, Jane's Sweet, 69
Whole Wheat Croissants, 71
Whole Wheat Danish Pastry Dough, Basic, 76
Whole Wheat Short Pastry, 27

Winter Compote, 98

Yeast Ring with Streusel Topping, 75
Yogurt
  Asparagus Yogurt Soufflé, 16
  Lassi (Yogurt Drink), 107
  Mocha Yogurt Loaf, 64
  Strawberry Yogurt Sauce, 54
  Yogurt Bread Starter, 68

Zewelwai (Onion Pie), 30
Zucchini
  Frittata Di Zucchine, 13
  Zucchini-Onion Pancakes Gratineés, 59
  Zucchini Quiche, 34

Credits and Acknowledgments

The following people contributed the recipes included in this book:

Sam Arnold
Paul Bhalla
Anthony Dias Blue
Marie-Aude Brooks and Nikko Pitanis
Mrs. William F. Buckley
Natalie Berkowitz and
    Judith Lebson
Sharon Cadwallader
Giovanni Caione, *Gritti Palace Hotel,*
    Venice, Italy
Mrs. John R. Drexel III
Frances Dunseth
Naomi French
Paul Gillette
Gerri Gilliland
Rhoda Gordon
Matty Goldberg
Marion Gorman
Geoffrey Holder
Barbara Horowitz
The Inverary Inn, Nova Scotia, Canada
Shari Karney
Lynne Kasper
Kay Koch
Margaret H. Koehler
Jean Kressy
Peter Kump
Louise Lamensdorf and
    Reni Steves
Rita Leinwand
Honey Lesser
John Loring
The Magnolia Hotel, Yountville,
    California, Owners Bruce and Bonnie
    Locken
Abby Mandel
Christina McClure
Perla Meyers

Jinx and Jefferson Morgan
Richard Nelson
Beatrice Ojakangas
Laurie Polansky
Sharon Puttmann
Constance and Brooke Stapleton
Doris Tobias
Jeremiah Tower
The Trellis, Williamsburg, Viginia
Jan Weimer
Anne Willan
Janet Yaseen

Additional text was supplied by:

Carol Field, *All About Coffee, All About
    Tea*
Rhoda Gordon, *Danish Pastry*
Lynne Kasper, *Pastry Primer*
Rita Leinwand, *Omelets, Steps to a
    Perfect Strudel Roll*
Honey Lesser, *Sourdough: Start Your
    Own*
Abby Mandel, *Basic Sorbet Techniques*
Jan Weimer, *Poached and Boiled Eggs,
    General Directions for Sausage
    Making and Cooking, Crepes*

Special thanks to:

Marilou Vaughan, *Editor, Bon Appétit*
William J. Garry,
    Managing Editor, Bon Appétit
Bernard Rotondo,
    Art Director, Bon Appétit
Leslie A. Dame,
    Editorial Assistant, Bon Appétit
Anthony P. Iacono,
    *Vice-President, Manufacturing,
    Knapp Communications Corporation*
Philip Kaplan,
    *Vice-President,
    Executive Graphics,
    Knapp Communications Corporation*

Patrick R. Casey,
    *Vice-President, Production
    Knapp Communications Corporation*
G. Dean Larrabee and Karen Legier,
    *Rights and Permissions Coordinators,
    Knapp Communications Corporation*
Maryanne Kibodeaux
Elaine Linden
June Gader
Sonsie Conroy

The Knapp Press
is a wholly owned subsidiary of
KNAPP COMMUNICATIONS CORPORATION
Chairman and Chief Executive Officer:
    Cleon T. Knapp
President: H. Stephen Cranston
Senior Vice-Presidents:
    Paige Rense *(Editor-in-Chief)*
    Everett T. Alcan *(Corporate Planning)*
    Rosalie Bruno *(New Venture
        Development)*
    John L. Decker *(Magazine Group
        Publisher)*
    Betsy Wood Knapp *(MIS Electronic
        Media)*
    L. James Wade, Jr. *(Finance)*

THE KNAPP PRESS

President: Alice Bandy; *Administrative
Assistant:* Beth Bell; *Senior Editor:*
Norman Kolpas; *Associate Editors:*
Jeff Book, Jan Koot, Sarah Lifton,
Pamela Mosher; *Assistant Editor:*
Taryn Bigelow; *Editorial Coordinator:*
Jan Stuebing; *Editorial Assistant:*
Nancy D. Roberts; *Art Director:* Paula
Schlosser; *Design Associates:* Robin
Murawski, Nan Oshin; *Production
Manager:* Larry Cooke; *Production
Coordinator:* Joan Valentine; *Financial
Manager:* Robert Groag; *Financial
Analyst:* Carlton Joseph; *Financial
Assistant:* Kerri Culbertson;
Fulfillment Services Manager: Virginia
Parry; *Marketing Manager:* Jan B. Fox;
Promotions Manager: Jeanie Gould;
Marketing Assistants: Dolores
Briqueleur, Joanne Denison; *Special
Sales:* Lynn Blocker; *Department
Secretaries:* Amy Hershman, Randy
Levin

This book is set in Sabon, a face designed by Jan Teischold in 1967 and based on early
fonts engraved by Garamond and Granjon.

Composition was on the Merganthaler Linotron 202 by Graphic Typesetting Service.

Series design by Paula Schlosser. Page layout by Robin Murawski.

Text stock: Allied Superior A.F. Offset, Basis 65. Color plate stock: Mead Northcote
Basis 70. Both furnished by WWF Paper Corporation West.

Color separations by NEC Incorporated.

Printing and binding by R.R. Donnelley and Sons.